THEN
JAPAN
& NOW

For more on books by William de Lange visit:
www.williamdelange.com

First edition, 2024

Published by TOYO PRess
Visit us at: **www.toyopress.com**

ISBN: 978-94-92722-447

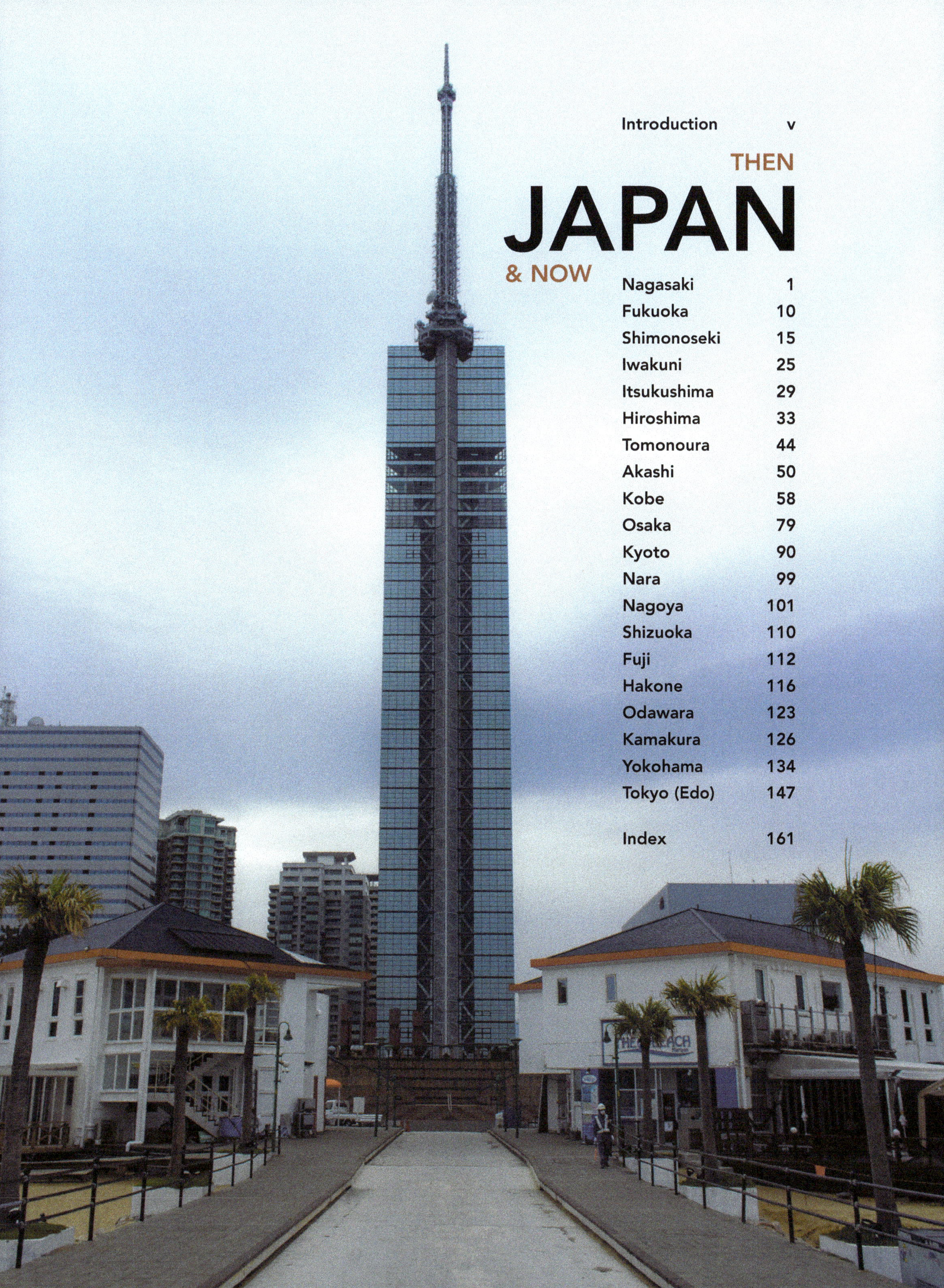

Tokyo
Yokohama
Hakone
Komakura
Fuji
Odawara
Nagoya
Shizuoka
Kyóto
Kobe
Nara
Akashi
Osaka
Hiroshima
Tomonoura
Iwakuni
Itsukushima
Shimonoseki
Fukuoka
Nagasaki

INTRODUCTION

The title of this book might equally have been *Japan: Now & Then*, for it is only now and then that one encounters the old Japan when traveling Japan, especially its cities. Most of the time one is trapped in the modern, high-tech version of Japan, a country that seems radically different from the country it was just over a century ago.

It is partly due to the massive Allied air raids of the Second World War that so much of late 19th-century Japan has vanished from the face of the earth. Far more buildings were destroyed and far more people were killed in the air raids conducted by the USAAF Bomber Command than in the immediate aftermath of the atomic bombing of Hiroshima. Thus, in one single air raid, codenamed Operation Meetinghouse II, conducted on the night of 9 to 10 March 1945, 279 (out of 346 departed) B29 Bombers released a total of 1,590.3 tonnes of (AN-M47 and AN-M69) incendiary bombs over Tokyo's densely populated Shitamachi area. Strong westerly winds fanned the ensuing flames into a firestorm that ravaged 41 km². In its wake, the Metropolitan Police Department reported the deaths of 83,793 citizens. At the end of the war, the total number of confirmed deaths in the more than thirty Tokyo air raids had reached 115,000, while the number of destroyed or damaged homes exceeded 850,000.

But it is not only Japan's war of aggression that (like in Germany) is to blame for the huge losses to its cultural heritage. That much was done on purpose is evinced by the Meiji Government's *Haijō-rei*, which oversaw the dismantlement of three-quarters of Japan's remaining castles. Not all were eventually lost. There were a number of valiant local efforts to preserve at least some of the old structures. At Inuyama Castle, for instance, where a number of former retainers saved the castle's keep. The same happened at Matsumae Castle, where the keep, main gate, and *goten* (the lord's residential palace), were spared, though they were forced to sell off the material and roof tiles of the remaining structures to support themselves. There were a few more happy exceptions, among them Hikone, Nagoya, and Himeji castles.

Another cause of much unnecessary loss of cultural heritage was the pernicious concept of *shin-butsu bunri* or 'the separation of Shintō and Buddhism.' During the Edo period, there had been an almost symbiotic relationship between the two religions. But in 1870, with a view to strengthen the Shintō religion and thereby support the State, the Meiji government seized on dormant sentiments that the two religions be separated. One of its side-effects was the resurgence of the *haibutsu-kishaku* movement, which advocated the expulsion of the non-native religion by 'abolishing Buddhism and destroying Shākyamuni. It is estimated that close to forty thousand temples were destroyed as a result. Many of their religious artifacts were bought by resident foreigners and shipped abroad, never to return again.

Much, then, has been lost. But much has been preserved, too. Every now and then one finds oneself catching one's breath, stunned by how well-preserved a place or building is, creating the impression that past and present perfectly overlap.

Note: Where necessary, maps indicate the vantage point from which a photograph was taken.

NAGASAKI

Dejima

Nagasaki's most historic piece of real estate is probably Dejima, an artificial island in the Bay of Nagasaki from which the Dutch were allowed to conduct their trade with Japan during its two-and-a-half century of isolation. That period ended during the middle of the 19th century, when due to Commodore Matthew Calbraith Perry's gunboat diplomacy, Japan saw itself forced to sign (unequal) trade treaties with a string of Western powers and open its ports to foreign ships.

When it was built, the fan-shaped island lay at the edge of town and at the foot of Nagasaki Bay. By now, it has been swallowed up; the city has encroached on the bay by another five hundred

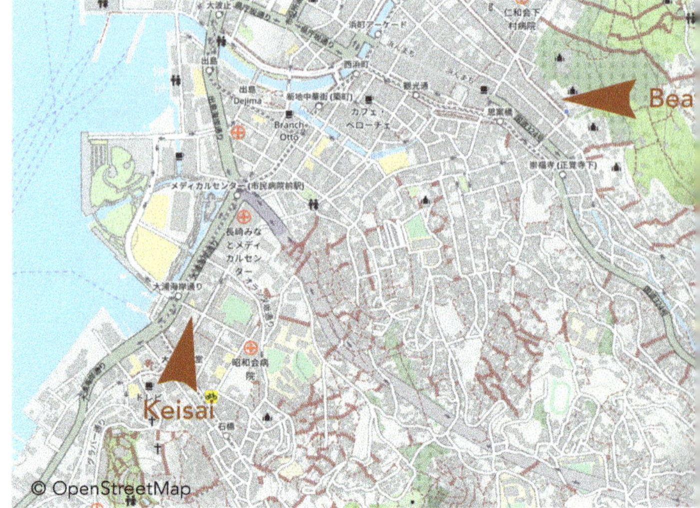

yards so that the Nagasaki Seaside Park now takes pride of place in overlooking the bay.

Dejima has gone through many iterations over the centuries. When the Dutch first moved in, in the spring of 1641, the island was populated by a dozen wooden buildings that resembled the kind of buildings found in other Dutch settlements around the world. They were made of wood—the Japanese authorities forbade the use of bricks—and had tiled roofs. Their number had doubled by the turn of the century but was halved again toward the end of the 18th century when, on 3 April 1798, a huge fire destroyed all the buildings on the west wing of the island, including the factor's quarters. The remainder was dismantled after the Dutch trading post closed in 1859. They had to make room for more modern buildings to accommodate foreign settlers and tourists. It is of this Dejima that the first photographs were taken during the *bakumatsu* period, the dying days of the Tokugawa shogunate.

One of them, taken in 1870 by Yoshio Keisai, depicts an island populated with colonial-style buildings, with double verandas. Keisai set up his camera on Glover-*zaka*, the northern slope of Mt. Nabekanmuri leading up to Glover House, the residence of the Scottish trader Thomas Glover. In the foreground, one can still see the wooden Matsugaeda Bridge across the Ōura River, which was replaced by a cast iron bridge during the Meiji period.

> **Yoshio Keisai** (1788–1866) was born into a family of physicians attached to the Dutch factory who also acted as interpreters. Following in his father's footsteps, he studied under the German physician Otto Gottlieb Johann Mohnike (1814–87), who helped introduce a cowpox vaccine, thus greatly contributing to the reduction of smallpox in Japan. Studying medicine at the Nagasaki Naval Training Center, Keisai developed an interest in photography, which he pursued under fellow physician-cum-photograper Matsumoto Ryōjun (1832–1907).

Another photographer to capture **Dejima** during this period was the Italian-British photographer Felice Beato, who had landed in Yokohama in 1863 and had come to Kyushu a year later to photograph the British military expedition against Shimonoseki. Arriving in Nagasaki in the early summer of 1865, he met up with fellow photographers like Ueno Hikoma. The latter had learned his craft under Johan Pompe van Meerdervoort, who taught chemistry at the **Nagasaki Naval Training Center**. Beato set up his camera atop Mt. Don, a few hundred meters east of Dejima Island. A present-day folk tale has it that the mountain derived its name from

a gun placement that was erected on its western slope at the turn of the century—the Japanese onomatopoeia '*doon*' is used to mimic the boom of a

cannon. In truth, the mountain derives its name from Japan's first Protestant church, which was erected at the foot of its western slope the year before

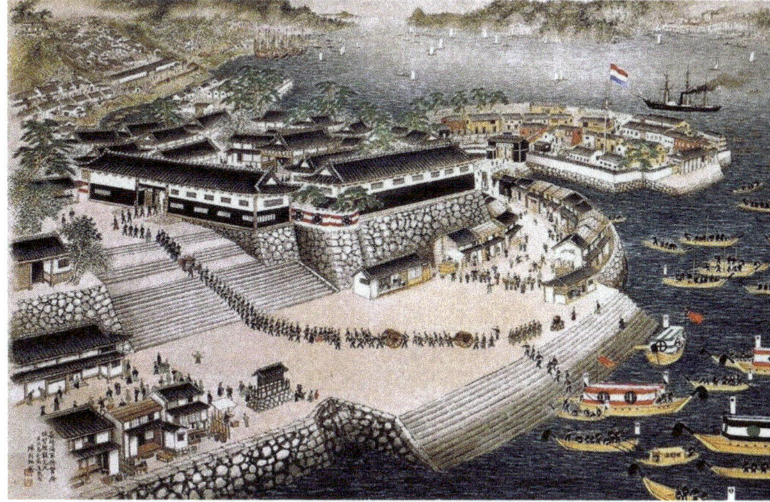

Beato arrived in Japan. Being used to refer to their predominantly Catholic missionaries as '*don*' or

'*don-sama*,' the Japanese converts tended to do the same with their Protestant ministers, and before long the site of their church also went by the name Don. Though it seems a hazy summer day in Beato's photograph, one can clearly make out the crescent shape of Dejima Island and the outlines of what would soon become Nagasaki's foreign settlement.

Felice Beato (1832–1909) was born in Venice, though it is not clear who his parents were. When Felice was still an infant, the Beatos, moved to Corfu, which at the time was part of the British protectorate of the Ionian Islands, resulting in Felice becoming a British subject. He had three siblings, one of them by the name of Antonio. Both brothers aspired to become professional photographers and, during their early years, worked together under a shared signature that read 'Felice Antonio Beato,' something that would cause a lot of confusion for later historians. Beato's career took off when he began to colaborate with the British photographer James Robertson (1813–88) and began traveling around the Mediterranean to meet the growing demand for souvenir pictures for tourists. In 1855 they explored a new avenue in photography when they traveled to Balaklava to capture the Crimean War. Beato next moved to India to photograph the aftermath of the Indian Rebellion of 1857. From there, he went to Hong Kong, where the Second Opium War was raging. In 1863, Beato entered perhaps the most productive phase in his career when he moved to Japan,  spending the next ten years photographing Japanese scenery, people, and life in general.

Kyoryūchi

When, in the wake of Japan's treaties with foreign powers, Hakodate, Yokohama, Shimoda, Kobe, and Nagasaki were opened to foreign ships, special so-called *gaikokujin kyoryūchi*, or 'foreign settlements,' were set up to accommodate the foreign settlers who arrived aboard them. Nagasaki, too, had its so-called *kyoryūchi*, a dedicated foreign settlement, which was situated along the eastern shore of Nagasaki Bay and was concentrated along both banks of the Ōura River.

One of the settlement's first main buildings was **Hotel Belle Vue**, which can be seen in the lower right-hand corner of a photograph taken by Enami Nobukuni during the early Meiji period. It was built by Matthew Green, the constable of the British con-

sulate in Nagasaki, who in 1861 leased a plot of land along the Ōura River to house the consulate. Building work began the next year, but shortly after its completion the consulate was moved and Green decided to turn the property into a hotel. He ran the hotel together with his wife, Mary Elizabeth. It seems of the two, Mary Elizabeth was the more tenacious, for when her husband upped and left without a trace in 1866, she continued to operate the hotel with the help of the Italian entrepreneur Carlo Napoleone Mancini. Hotel Belle Vue was Japan's first Western-style hotel. With rooms that could be had at $21 a week and meals at just $1, it became a hit with foreign businessmen and tourists who wanted to see the sights.

By the time Nobukuni took his photograph, many more Western-style buildings had sprung up near the Ōura River, among them a string of foreign consulates, a branch office of the Honkong-Shanghai Bank, and an International Club. They catered to the growing number of foreign residents who took up living in their own Western-style hous-

es that populated the area, one of the first and most luxurious being Thomas Glover's mansion at the top of Glover-*zaka*. The settlement's main street became **Matsuebashi**-*dōri*, a pleasant avenue that started out at the foot of Oranda-*zaka*, or Dutch Slope, and crossed the Ōura River at the Benten

Bridge, just a few dozen yards from where it poured into Nagasaki Bay.

Hotel Belle Vue closed its doors in 1920. It had operated for more than half a century, its lifespan roughly coinciding with that of Nagasaki's foreign settlement. The unequal treaties that had led to its formation had been abolished and jurisdiction over the area returned to the Japanese authorities. While foreigners were now free to settle in other parts of the city, the area remained a hub of foreign trade up until the outbreak of the Pacific War.

Enami Nobukuni (1859–1929) was born in Tokyo and learned his craft under Ogawa Kazumasa. To pursue his career, Nobukuni moved to Yokohama in 1892 and opened up a studio along its bustling Benten-*dōri*, just a few doors away from yet another Japanese photographer by the name of Tamamura Kōzaburō (1856–1923). The two men began working together, becoming prolific producers of images of scenic beauty that were reproduced in their thousands and were not only popular in Japan but also found their way to American publishers of photographic albums. Nobukuni's studio was lost in the fires that destroyed much of Tokyo and Yokohama in the wake of the 1923 earthquake.

The studio was rebuilt and when, a few years later, Nobukuni passed away at the age of seventy, it was taken over by his son, Tamotsu.

Ishibashi-gun

Another historic part of Nagasaki was the so-called Ishibashi-*gun* or the 'ston`e bridge group.' It was a collection of stone-arch bridges that spanned

Below: The Megane-*bashi* photographed by Felice Beato

Right: The Megane-*bashi* today

Nagasaki's Nakashima-*kawa*, a river that springs forth on the eastern slope of Mt. Hōka, northeast of Nagasaki, and ends its journey as the moat separating Dejima from the mainland. For hundreds of years, Nagasaki prided itself on its stone-arch bridges, perhaps the largest number to span a single city river in Japan into the 20th century. Until 1982, that is, when, between the 23rd and the 25th of July, a heavy cloudburst over the Nagasaki area released a deluge of water that reached 187mm per hour at its peak. It caused the Nakashima River to flood much of the downtown area and submerged its bridges in a torrent that swept all before

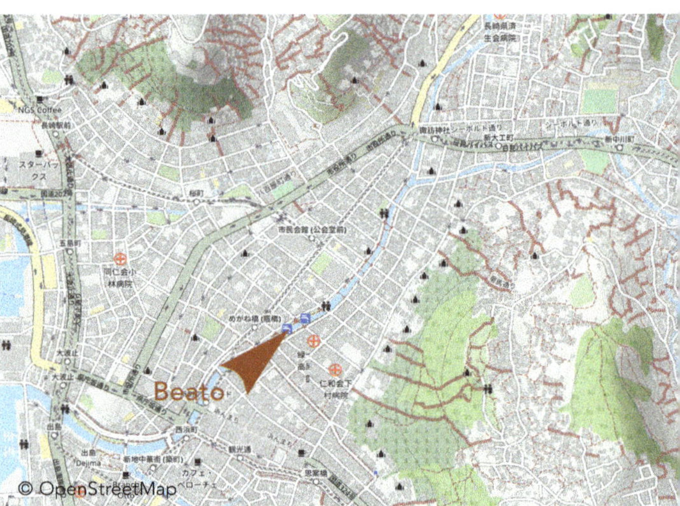

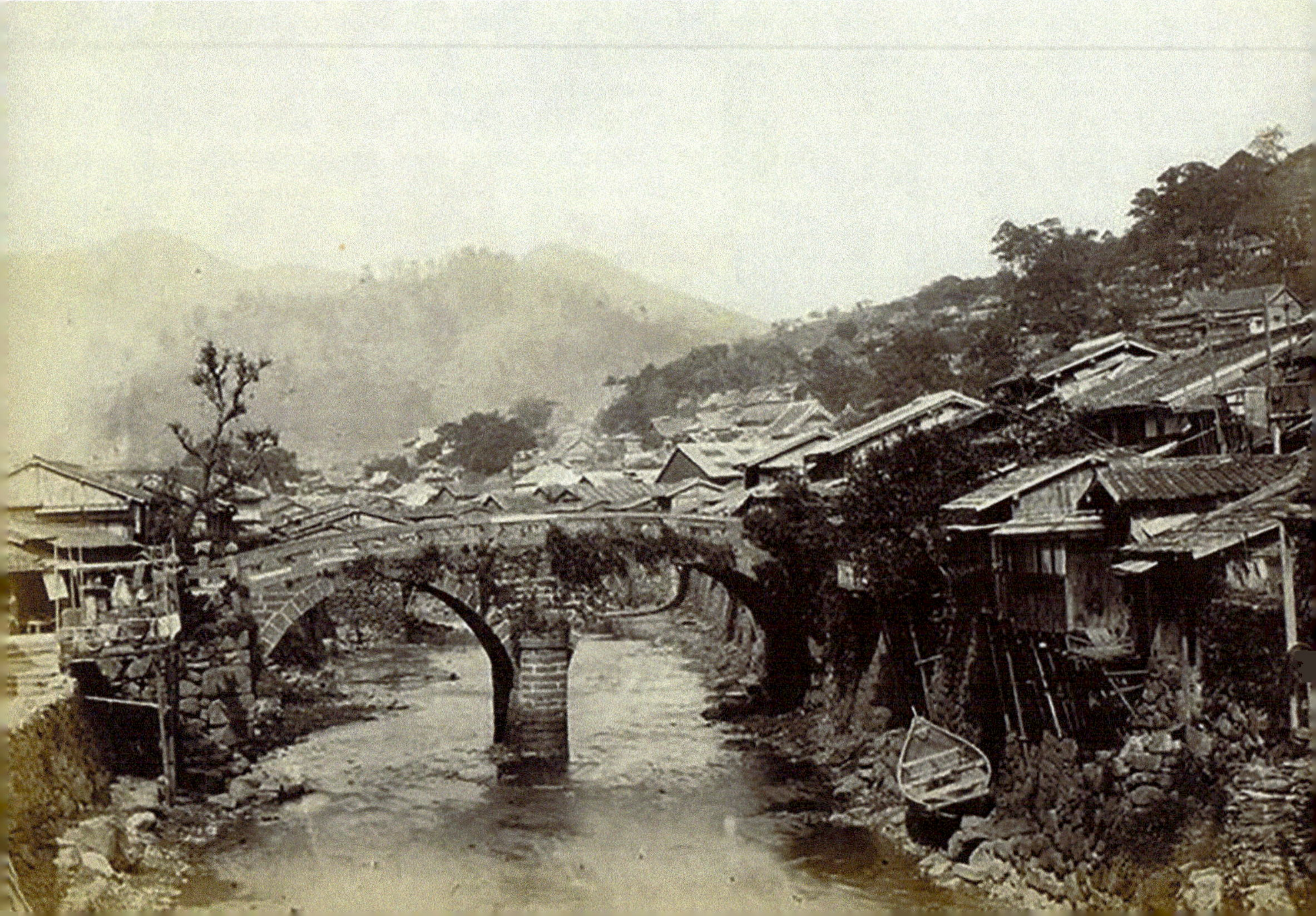

it. Seven of the river's stone-arch bridges—the Higashi Shin-*bashi*, the Susukihara-*bashi*, the Ichiran-*bashi*, the Furumachi-*bashi*, the Amigasa-*bashi*, the Ōide-*bashi*, and the Amida-*bashi*—were lost forever.

Only one bridge, the Megane-*bashi*, which straddles the river a few hundred yards upstream from Dejima Island, survived. Though part of its west-bank surface was washed away, the bridge's arches remained intact, despite being submerged in the torrent for more than a day. It was built by Mokusu Myojō, a Chinese monk attached to the Kōfuku Temple, which sits on a ridge overlooking the river from the east. Erected in 1634, it is (next to the Tennyo-*bashi* of Okinawa's Shuri Castle) the oldest surviving stone-arch bridge in Japan and was designated an Important Cultural Property in 1960.

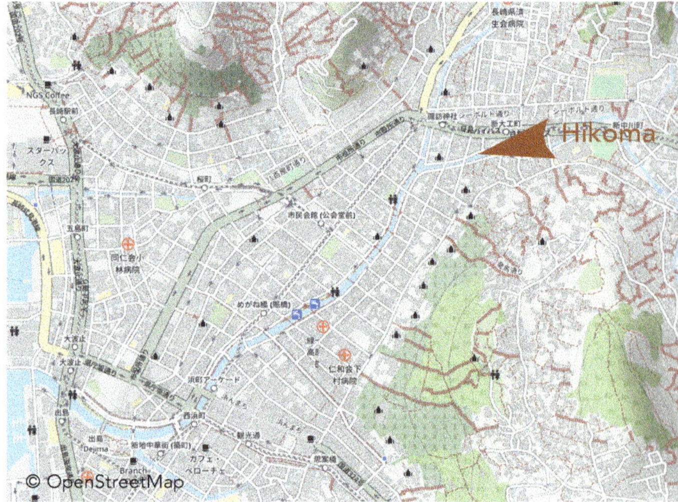

The Amida Bridge, the penultimate bridge across the Nakashima River before it turned south-ward toward the Bay of Nagasaki, was first pho-

NAGASAKI – Ishibashi-gun

tographed in 1872 by Ueno Hikoma. Hikoma was a native of Nagasaki and one of Japan's early photographers, whose studio stood a stone's throw upriver from the bridge. Through the bridge, one can clearly see the Kōrai-*bashi*. It is clear from Hikoma's picture that the river was used as a source of water, (though probably not for drinking) as wooden tubs are scattered around on the rocks and boulders in the riverbed. Not a soul can be seen in the riverbed, but this is probably due to the photograph's long exposure time. One person, sitting in front of the small structure atop the right bank sat still enough to be captured. The bridge was built in 1690 by a wealthy Nagasaki merchant by the name of Sonoyama Zenji, who also paid for its construction.

Initially, the bridges across the Nakajima River did not carry any names but were simply numbered, the Amida Bridge being number 1. This, however, led to such confusion that a Nagasaki

scholar by the name of Nishi Dōsen (1836–1913) was asked to give them names. The Amida Bridge got its name from a small temple dedicated to Amida Buddha, which stood on the south bank of the river. The Megane-*bashi* earned its name from its middle pillar, which divides the bridge into two semi-circular arches, causing it to resemble a pair of glasses, hence Dōsen named it 'Spectacle Bridge.' The Kōrai-*bashi*, or Korea Bridge, gave access to the Shinkōrai Township and was built in 1652 by the same Chinese monk attached to the Kōfuku Temple who built the Megane-*bashi*.

Ueno Hikoma (1838–1904) learned the rudiments of his profession under Johan Pompe van Meerdervoort, a Dutch instructor attached to the Nagasaki Naval Training Center. Van Meerdervoort was able to instruct his students in the science of chemistry, but his attempts to capture things on plate generally met with failure. It was only with the arrival in Nagasaki of the Swiss photographer Piere Rossier (1828–86), who instructed a large number of Japanese students in the art of photography, that Hikoma really mastered his craft. In this, he was supported by his father, a local scholar who had purchased Japan's first daguerreotype camera for Shimazu Nariakira, the *daimyō* of Satsuma. Hikoma, who also met and worked with the renowned Italian-British photographer Felice Beato during the latter's stay in Nagasaki in 1865, went on to have a distinguished career  as a photographer, exhibiting his work at the Vienna World Exposition of 1873 and the World Columbian Exposition of 1893.

FUKUOKA

Momochi-hama

One of Fukuoka City's many historic sites is what was known as Momochi-*hama* or Momochi Beach. The name Momochi derives from the time the area was just a vast tidal flat. At that time, people could freely roam in all wind directions as they pleased so that, over time, hundreds of crisscrossing trails began to leave their impression on the area's sparse vegetation. They were known as the Momo no Michi or the Hundred Roads. Over time, the name contracted into Momochi, a name that stuck up until today.

The beach in front of what was then still called **Hakata** has a significance to the Japanese that is on a par with those at Normandy must have had

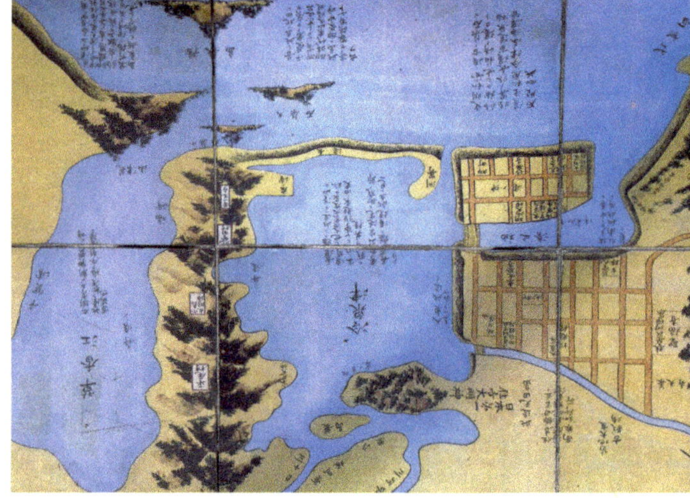

to the Germans during the Second World War, though luckily for the Japanese, the outcome was quite different. It was on Hakata's beaches that, on 19 November 1274, Japanese samurai faced a huge fleet of Kublai Kahn's Mongol hordes. It was a touch-and-go situation. After a long day of intense fighting, the Japanese army was forced to retreat, back to the stronghold of Mizu, some ten miles inland, where they prepared to make a last stand. But by then, the Mongol generals had already decided to retreat. Why exactly is unclear, though one of them was gravely wounded, their men sustained heavy losses, and heavy winds damaged and sunk a third of their fleet.

Kublai Kahn's second attempt at invading the Japanese Isles fared even worse. This time two fleets crossed the Tsushima Straits in the early summer of 1281. They were to converge at Iki Island, some thirty sea miles west of Hakata, but the commanders of the first fleet to reach the island refused to wait. They split their fleet in two and proceeded to attack both Hakata and the southern tip of Japan's main island of Honshū. But this time the Japanese were prepared. They had erected stone walls at all major landing sites, including Hakata Bay, while long stakes barred their ships from entering the mouths of the Kai and Muromi rivers that poured into the bay. Unable to land, the invaders withdrew to Noko-*shima*, the island at the center of the bay, but here, too, they were menaced by the Japanese, who launched repeated raids against them with small vessels. Again, it was the elements that came to the Japanese rescue. On the 15th and 16th of August, a devastating typhoon tore through the bay, scattering the Mongol fleet and sinking hundreds of its ships. When news of the Mongol defeat reached the then-capital of Kamakura, it was hailed as a sign the Japanese gods had delivered them. They had sent heavenly winds to assist the valiant warriors in repelling the invaders. From then

on, the storms that had saved them were known as *kamikaze*, or 'divine winds.'

The stakes and stone walls, too, played an important role in repelling the invaders. Sections of those walls are still scattered through Fukuoka city, tracing the former outline of the bay during the Kamakura period. They now cut straight through the heart of present-day Fukuoka City, which skirts the crescent-shaped bay but has encroached on it by several hundreds of meters. One section is preserved in the basement of the Hakata Elementary School in Fukuoka's downtown Kamigofuku Township. Another, much longer and restored section, still guards the beach at the **Ikonomatsubara Forest Park**, some forty-five minutes and nine stops west along Fukuoka's Airport Line.

During the early Edo period, when the country was at peace and faced no major outside threats,

the lord of Fukuoka Castle, Kuroda Nagamasa (1568–1623), ordered Momoji Beach to be lined with pine trees in an effort to limit erosion. As a result, the bay in front of his stronghold received

Below: Momiji Beach during the Taishō period

Right: Fukuoka Tower

a beautiful shoreline lined with a dense forest of fragrant pines. As a result the area also became known as the Momoji-*matsubara* or the Momoji Pine Grove. The scenery was even further enhanced when, in 1666, Nagamasa's grandson, Mitsuyuki (1628–1707), ordered the Momiji Hachiman-*gū* at Hashimoto, a village that lay some five kilometer upstream along the Muromi River, to be dismantled and re-erected at Takatori, right amid the pine forest his grandfather had planted.

It was during the heady Taishō era, but also the impoverished post-war years, that the beach in front of Fukuoka became the scene of one thing

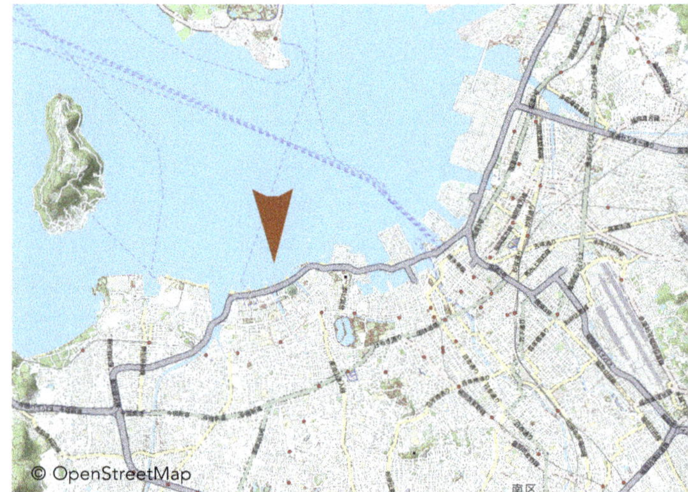

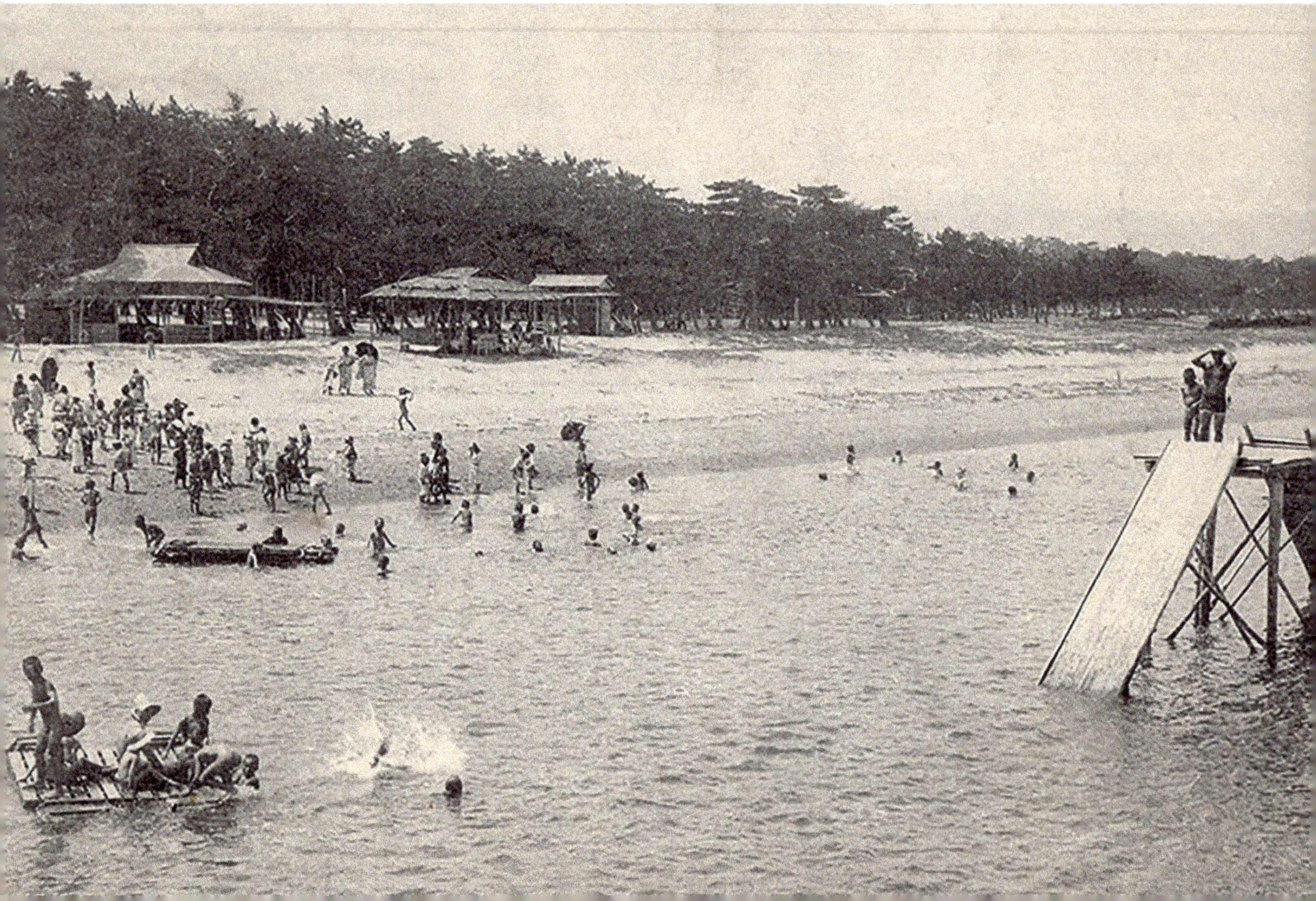

each of its citizens could indulge in: a dip in the sea. The name Momoji Beach became synonymous with fun and laughter, of children cavorting in the water and building sand castles. Adults could rent a small sailing boat and sail over to Noko Island. A wooden pier was built for daring young boys and girls to dive from, while their parents looked on from under the shade of the pines. At the mouth of the Muromi River, older citizens, who had experienced the war years and had known hunger, could be found hunting for *asari*, the small by delicious 'littleneck clams,' or prodding the sharp end of their sunshades into the wet sand to force out a *mategai*, or 'razor clam.' It was a place of untrammeled enjoyment, both for young and old.

Today, one would have a hard time finding even a trace of Momoji Beach. Large swathes of reclaimed land have made the city encroach on the bay, while high-rise city projects have replaced the fragrant pine grove. Now the former shoreline of Momoji Beach lies half a kilometer inland from what has been renamed the Momochi Seaside Park. The park, too, has a small stretch of beach, but it is man-made and no longer lined with pine trees so bulldozers have to be called in to counteract the threat of erosion. Halfway along the beach, a pier connects the mainland to an artificial island harboring the Marizon Beach Pavilion. There the happy few can book a table at an expensive restaurant, go shopping in its high-end mall, or tie the knot at its American-style wedding palace. Guarding over it all is not a stone wall but the steel and glass structure of Fukuoka Tower, a skyscraper from whose Scenic Observation Deck one can gaze down and marvel at the city's modern-day accomplishments.

SHIMONOSEKI

Kameyama Hachiman-gū

Kameyama means Mt. Turtle. Some say the hill on which Shimonoseki's eponymous shrine stands resembled the shell of a turtle; others claim it was the many turtles who inhabited the hill that gave it its name. The shrine dates back to the middle of the ninth century, when a Buddhist monk by the name Gyōkyō moored his boat at the hill, which was then still a small island barely connected to the mainland. An itinerant monk from Nara's Shingon-*shū* Daian Temple, Gyōkyō was on his way back from Kyushu when, touched by the area's tranquility, he interrupted his journey to spend

some time on the island in quiet contemplation. It was the small abode his followers built to give him shelter that became a place of pilgrimage and

reverence for his local followers and the forerunner of the present shrine.

As can be seen in this old **painting**, already during the Edo period, the small island on which the shrine stood had been joined to the mainland, and

the shoreline was reinforced by boulders. The small building immediately in front of the elevated shrine, just to the right, is marked out as a *bandokoro*, or

'guard house.' Such guardhouses were installed by Japan's feudal lords to control important strong points in their domain. Shimonoseki was under the rule of the Chōshū domain, which was controlled by the powerful Mōri clan throughout its existence.

The **guard house** can still be seen in the photograph Felice Beato took of the shrine in 1864 while on his way to his photographer friends in Nagasaki. By the time Uchida Kuichi took his photograph during the early Meiji period, the guard house had been dismantled, as Japan's domains had been dissolved and there was no longer any need for such structures.

But the shrine's wide flight of steps still led down to a small terrace immediately abutting the straits. This, too, was to change within a few decades, for the sea in front of the shrine was reclaimed during the 1890s, creating the Karato Township with its now famous Katato Fish Market. Today, the Kameyama Hachiman-*gū*'s wide flight of stairs no longer leads down to the water but to the black tarmac of National Route No. 9, which follows almost the entire northern shore of the straits.

Uchida Kuichi (1844–75) was born in Nagasaki and became an orphan while still in his infancy. He was adopted by his uncle, a physician who had been trained at the Naval Training Center. Kuichi, too, became a student, studying chemistry under Johan Pompe van Meerdervoort alongside Ueno Hikoma and others. Like Hikoma, Kuichi also took up photography, honing his skills under the guidance of Maeda Genzō (1831–1906). In 1864, Kuichi moved to Osaka, where he opened a studio specializing in portrait photography. Many of his customers at the time were famous *geisha* and *kabuki* actors. Two years later, he moved to Yokohama; and a year later still, to Tokyo, where he opened a studio in Asakusa. The high point in Kuichi's career came in 1872, when he was commissioned by the Imperial Household to take por-

Below: The Akama-*jingū* in 1936, less than a decade before its burned down

Right: The Akama-*jingū* today

traits of Emperor Meiji and Empress Haruko in court dress and everyday robes. The next year,

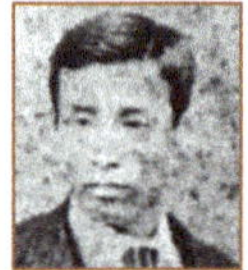

he took another photograph of the emperor, this time in military uniform, which was selected as the official imperial portrait.

Akama-jingū

Perhaps even more famous than the Kameyama Hachiman-*gū* is the Akama-*jingū*. It stands on equally elevated grounds, just a few hundred yards eastward along the coast. It is already clearly visible in the above painting. It should be, for if we may believe the historical records, it was founded in 859, the exact same year as its sister shrine down the road. And like its sister shrine, it too claims to have been founded by Gyōkyō when he passed through Shimonoseki. Akama means 'red gate,' a name the temple derived from the huge red entrance gate that guards the shrine.

Though the word *jingū* denotes 'Shintō Shrine,' the complex used to be a Buddhist temple known as the Amida-*ji*. It is widely believed the temple was built to house the remains of Antoku, the young prince of royal blood who famously drowned during the Gempei War's closing sea battle at Dan no Ura in 1185. It is only a fifteen-minute stroll north along the shore's embankment to the site of the historic site of Dan no Ura, but no remains of an infant have ever been found at the shrine, nor,

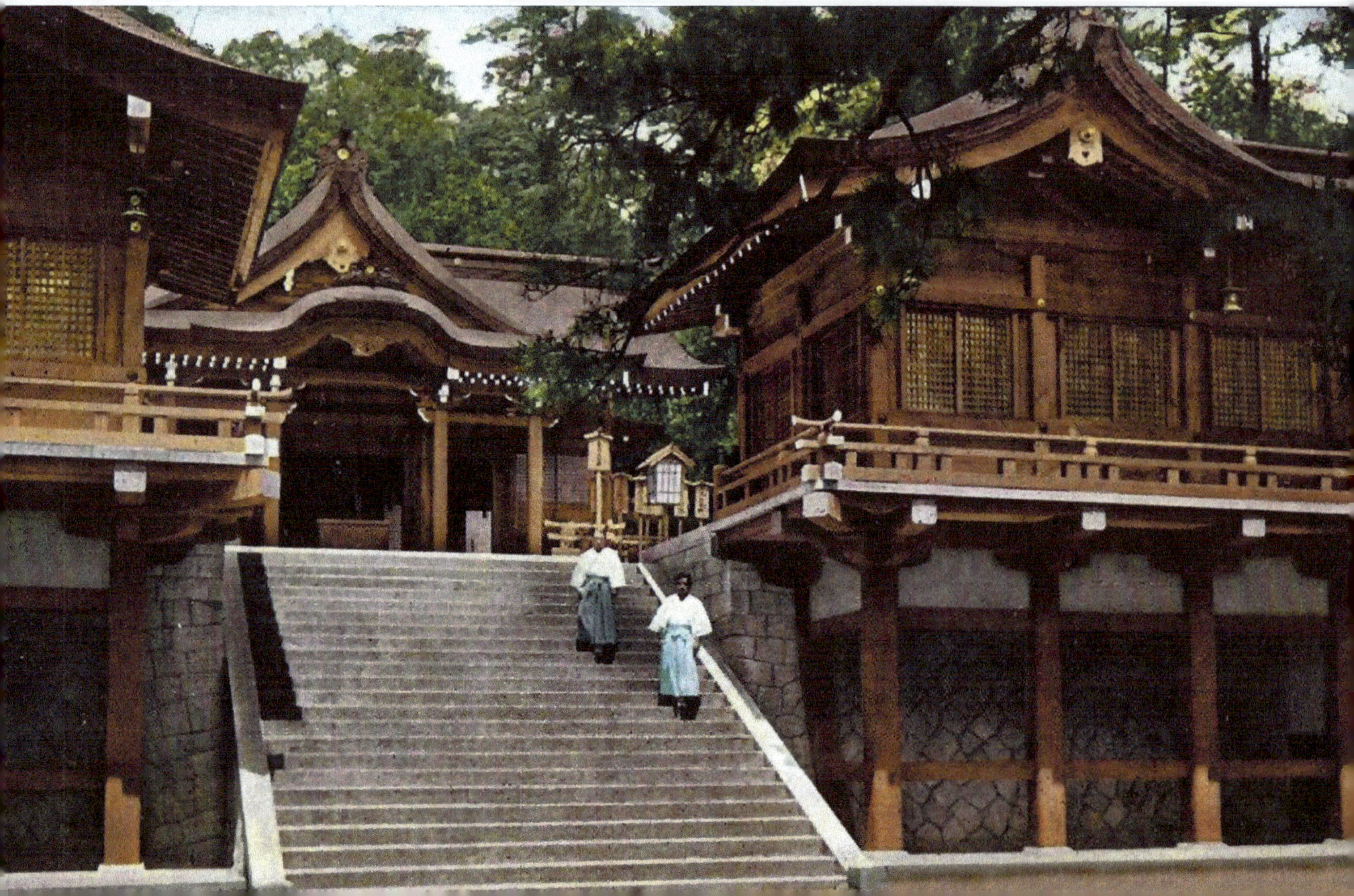

for that matter, at any of other places that claim the honor. It was probably because, like the Kameyama Hachiman-*gū*, the temple was dedicated to the God of War, that six years later, a Hall for the repose of Antoku's spirit was erected at the temple by imperial decree.

During the 1870s the Meiji government seized the temple's association with the Imperial family to change it into a Shintō shrine. The motive behind the move was their policy of *shinbutsu bunri*, a dormant Edo period movement that advocated the 'separation of Shintō and Buddhism.' One reason why the Meiji leaders chose to adopt the policy was to curtail the wealth and power of the Buddhist church. The other was to strengthen the Shintō religion. Being an indigenous religion that fostered reverence for the Emperor, it proved a perfect vehicle to boost the desired love of country. Thousands of temples were closed, their grounds confiscated, their monks forced to return to secular life.

The shrine that can be seen in the color photograph from 1936 (author unknown) no longer exists.

It was destroyed during Allied air raids on 29 June and 2 July 1945, when two squadrons of B-29 Superfortresses dropped some 700 tons of incendiary bombs over Shimonoseki.

The present shrine is a reconstruction dating back to 1964. Done in the gaudy colors of Chinese temples, it lacks the exquisite sobriety of the original. Yet because of its historic significance, the shrine on a so-called *beppyō*, a 'special list' that included famous shrines like Tsurugaoka Hachiman-*gū* in Kamakura, the Atsuta-*jingū* in Nagoya, and the Itsukushima-*jinja* on the eponymous island.

Maeda Gun Battery

The guard house in front of the Kameyama Hachiman-*gū* captured on plate by Felice Beato in 1864 wasn't there just for show. Just one year earlier, the domain's ruler, Mōri Takachika (1819–71), had ordered his retainers to fire on any foreign ship passing through the straits. He did so in response to an imperial edict to 'expel the barbarians,' yet in direct contravention to the Tokugawa *bakufu*'s policy to open Japan up to the West. Indeed, it may well have been from this very guardhouse that, on 8 July 1863, one of his retainers with a sharp eye spotted the French naval dispatch steamer *Kien Chan* making its way up the straits. By the time the vessel was abreast of Shimonoseki, she came under fire of several gun batteries. Two of them, situated at slightly different elevations, were located at Maeda, just east of the strait's narrow. There was also one atop Mt. Kameyama. Not only the French qualified as barbarians. Two weeks earlier, on 25 June, the American merchant vessel SS *Pembroke* had already come under fire from Chōshū's guns while at anchor on the other side of the straits, and this while a number of the 8-inch Dahlgren guns had been gifted to the domain by the United States. Even vessels of the Dutch, who had been teaching students from Chōshū in Western ways of warfare at the Nagasaki Naval Training Center, were considered fair game. On 11 June, despite having spoken to the *Kien Chan*, the Dutch warship *Medusa* steamed up the straits, convinced she would be safe from attack. She was not. Shimonoseki's gun batteries fired more than thirty shells into the vessel. Her captain, François de Casembroot (1817–95), responded in kind, but fearful of endangering the life of the Dutch Consul General, who was on board, he withdrew, incurring heavy damage, as well as nine casualties.

The inevitable response came swiftly. On 16 July, the American frigate USS *Wyoming* entered the straits and engaged the Chōshū fleet for close to two hours. Four days later, two French warships took Shimonoseki under fire.

The showdown came the next year when, on 5 September, a squadron of nine British, four Dutch, and three French warships carrying some two thousand troops sailed up the eastern entrance to the

The Straits of
Shimonoseki today

straits. The squadron was led by Admiral Augustus Leopold Kuper aboard the flagship *Euryalus*. With him on the flagship was Felice Beato, who had been hired as the punitive expedition's official photographer. By the end of the next day, most of Chōshū's gun batteries had been silenced. By the 8th they had been dismantled, too. But not before Beato took a photograph of the British forces in possession of the Maeda gun battery. The image was probably taken on the day after the battle, for the marines in the picture seem relaxed and jolly and evidently confident that they're out of danger.

The Maeda gun battery has been preserved and is now a Designated National Historic Site. A notice board explains that the guns had a sweep that ranged from the Suonada on the east, all the way to the strait's narrow toward the west. The view from the placement today is still magnificent, though part of it is obscured by a hideous eight-story apartment complex.

SHIMONOSEKI – Maeda Gun Battery

IWAKUNI

Kintai-kyō

Perhaps Japan's most famous—and certainly most beautiful—bridge is Iwakuni's Kintain-*kyō*, or Kintai Bridge. Straddling the Nishiki River, shortly before it pours into the Inland Sea at Iwakuni City, it pro-vided access to Iwakuni Castle. When it was first built, in 1608, the stronghold sat on Mt. Yoko, a headland in the curve of the Nishiki River. But only seven years later, its lord Kikkawa Hiroie ordered his men to tear it down again. The reason behind his destructive act was the Tokugawa *bakufu*'s *Ikkoku Ichijō-rei* of 1615, or the 'One Country One Castle Ordinance. Under it, a lord was allowed

only one castle per domain. He need not have bothered. It so happened that Hiroie was merely a vassal of the powerful Mōri clan, who already

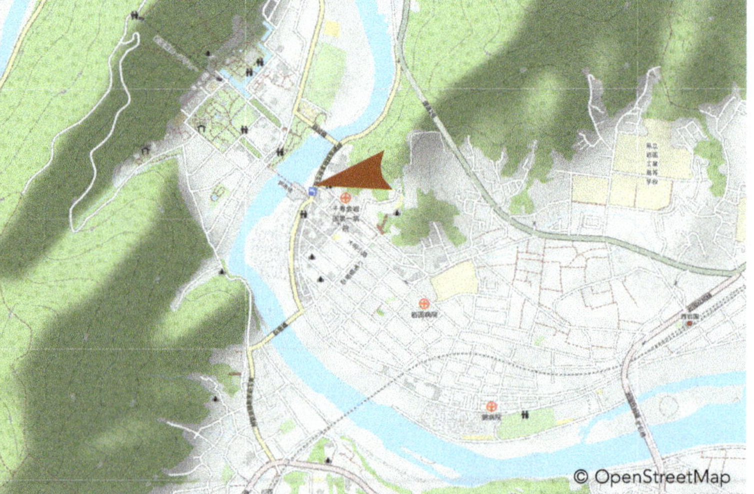

had Hagi Castle in Nagato Province (northern Yamaguchi Prefecture) as their headquarters. Iwakuni Castle stood in the neighboring province

the Mōri ruled two provinces and were therefore entitled to two castles. But by then, all the structures atop Mt. Yoko had already been dismantled. Only the residential area at the foot of the mountain was left intact.

So was the wooden bridge across the Nishiki River, which resembled wooden bridges elsewhere in the country in that its deck as well as its supporting structure were made of wood. Situated in Japan's western region, which is annually visited by fierce typhoons, the bridge was regularly washed away until, in 1673, the castle's third lord, Kikkakwa Hiroyoshi, ordered his chief architect Kodama Kurōemon to **design a bridge** that could withstand the river's mighty torrents. Kurōemon designed a bridge of five mortise-and-tenon arches (*seri-mochi*) made from zelkova beams supported by stone piers.

Kurōemon's first attempt proved flawed, for only a year later, the stone piers that supported the

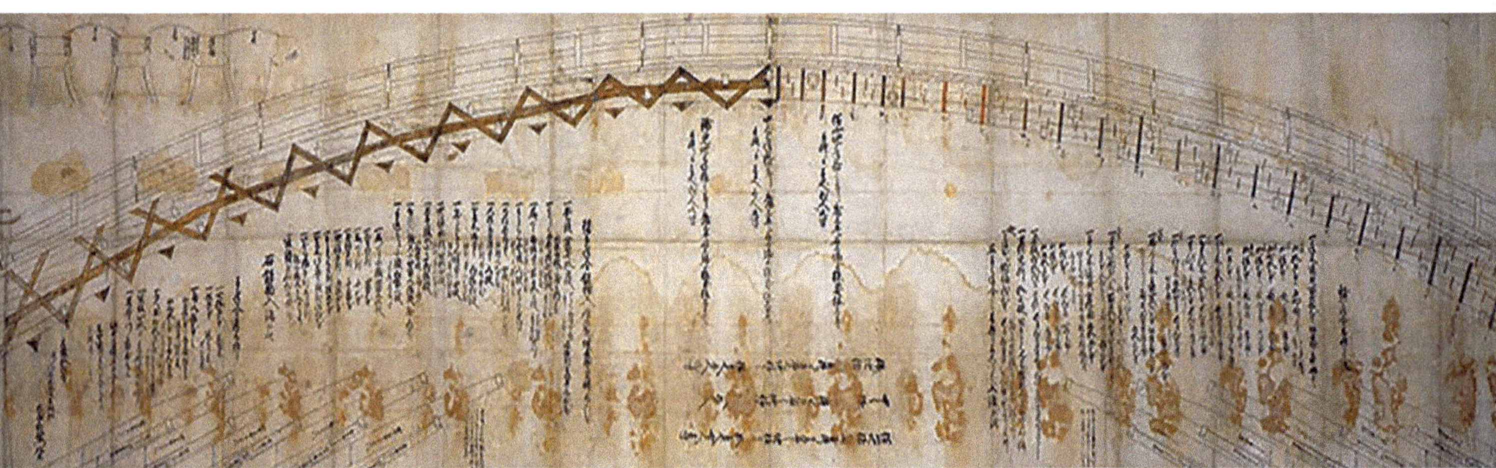

of Suō, which meant that it complied with the conditions of the *bakufu*'s ordinance. The *bakufu* acknowledged as much when it pronounced that

new wooden structure collapsed during another typhoon, and the whole structure was washed away again. But Kurōemon wasn't deterred and set about

designing a new bridge that would survive the wildest torrents. Its new stone piers were wider, and the wooden structure even sturdier. To prevent it from weakening through wear and tear, a tax was levied on the domain's retainers and merchants to rebuild the bridge's central arches every two decades and the outer two every four decades.

For almost two hundred years, only the lord and his vassals were allowed to cross the bridge; Iwakuni's common folk had to ford the river at its shallows when the water was low and cross it by boat when the water was high. It took until 1868 and the abolishment of Japan's feudal system before they, too, were allowed to tread its deck. The bridge itself withstood the test of time for more than two-and-a-half centuries. But fate struck on 14 September 1950, when typhoon Kezia struck the region and washed the bridge away a second time. This time around, it was through no fault of its architect. Poor maintenance during the war years had weakened the bridge's wooden structures, while large-scale felling of pine trees to produce pine oil had reduced the upriver region's ability to retain water. Only its central three arches were carried away by the torrents. And here, too, the bridge functioned exactly as Kurōemon had envisioned, for he had designed the arches in such a way that they would be lifted out of their sockets when the water rose too high in order to spare the rest of the bridge.

Good wood was hard to come by, and so the municipality designated a special stretch of local forest for the cultivation of the precious zelkova. It was this wood that was used in the bridge's large-scale overhaul between 2001 and 2004 to the tune of ¥2.6 billion (roughly $17 million).

IWAKUNI – Kintai-kyō

ITSUKUSHIMA

Itsukushima-jinja

The island of Itsukushima, which flanks the north-west shore of Hiroshima Bay, is cherished in Japan as one of its three most celebrated scenic sights. It was the Edo Confucianist Hayashi Gahō (1618–80) who came up with the concept, the other two sites being the island cluster in Matsushima Bay near Sendai and the Amanohashidate Sandbar in Miyazu Bay.

What made the island of Itsuku (*shima* means 'island') so attractive to the philosopher was not only its idyllic setting along the coast of Hiroshima Bay but also the many shrines and temples that populated the island. It is for this reason that the island is also known as Miya-*jima* or 'Shrine Island.'

Most famous among them is undoubtedly the Itsukushima-*jinja*, which is widely believed to have been founded by Taira no Kiyomori, whose machinations at court helped pave the way to the ascendancy of the warrior class during the late Heian period.

In truth, the shrine was founded almost half a millennium earlier. Legend has it that, in 593, a local bigwig by the name of Saeki no Kuramoto had a vision in which the female goddess Ichikishima-*hime* told him to erect a shrine in her name. Kuramoto did as he was told, but the name soon changed to Itsuku, which means so much as 'to worship,' or 'to enshrine.'

Taira no Kiyomori's association with the shrine goes back to his time as governor of Aki Province, which covered the western part of Hiroshima Prefecture. The layout of today's shrine is largely

the work of Kiyomori, who built a shrine that extended over the water in one of the island's coves and, when the tide was out, erected a large *torii* at the entrance of the cove.

With the Taira's demise in the sea battle at Dan no Ura, the shrine continued to receive the patronage of their victors, the Minamoto. It did not save it from being destroyed by fire twice in short succession, first in 1207, and again in 1223. It was duly rebuilt, and it was this version, built during the middle if the 13th century that has largely survived to this day.

It was almost destroyed by fire again, this time on purpose, when, during the early Meiji years, the government supervisor in charge of shrines and temples discovered that the ceremonies that were being conducted at the shrine's main hall had a distinctive Buddhist flavor. This ran counter to the government's policy of *shinbutsu bunri*, the strict separation of Shintō and Buddhism that also was to affect Shimonoseki's Amida Temple as well as countless other temples and shrines. De main hall's design, too, had 'faults.' It was built in the *shinden-zukuri* tradition, a style of architecture used for the palaces of noblemen. It lacked the ornamental forked finials (*chigi*), the bargeboards (*hafu*) extending beyond the roof's ridge line; nor did it feature the log-like elements (*katsuogi*) set perpendicular to the roof's ridgepole (*kō-ita*). The best option, he advised, was to simply burn the structure down to the ground and start afresh. His was a typical early-Meiji-period attitude that would spell the tragic end of hundreds of temples, shrines, monasteries, and castles.

Luckily the shrine's head priest had other plans. Connected in high places, he appealed directly to members of the Meiji government and managed to persuade them to save his centuries-old shrine.

By way of concession, the structures were stripped of all paint and Buddhist images, while the roofs received the features to make them resemble the sober *shinmei-zukuri* style for which the Ise Shrine is famous. Thus it is that photographs from that period all feature the prominent forked finials.

It only took a few decades for the authorities to realize their folly and for the 'restorations' to be reversed: during the Taishō era, the fake *chigi* and *katsuogi* were binned and the structures received a new coat of the original bright, orange-red paint.

Nowadays, the Itsukushima Shrine attracts more than three million visitors each year. Among them are also Japanese politicians who like to impress visiting foreign dignitaries with one of Japan's three major scenic sites, often after they have first paid their respects at the Atomic Bomb Dome in Hiroshima's Peace Memorial Park.

ITSUKUSHIMA – Itsukushima-jinja

HIROSHIMA

Genbaku Dōmu

Hiroshima's most iconic building is a ruin. It is the shell of what was once the Hiroshima-*ken* Bussan Chinretsu-*kan*, Hiroshima Prefecture's Product Exhibition Hall. It was built in 1915 at the then astronomic cost of ¥190.000, which would now amount to roughly $3 million. It was built to showcase the products of Hiroshima's industry, an industry that had received a massive impetus as a result of the Russo-Japanese was of 1904. Its architect was Jan Letzel (1880–1925), a Czech who had moved to Japan in 1907 and founded an architectural bureau. He went on to design some forty buildings, includ-

ing Tokyo's German embassy (which stood at the site of the present Diet) and, together with Georg de Lalande, Kobe's Oriental Hotel. Work on the Product Exhibition Hall was begun in January 1914 and completed on 5 April of the next year. It opened to the public four months later.

For the next three decades the structure continued to serve its intended purpose: to promote the products of Hiroshima's considerable industrial complex. As Japan rapidly geared up to war during the 1930s, the exhibitions became more and more focused on the military products that rolled off Hiroshima's assembly lines, at first for the occupation of Manchuria, then for the war against China, and finally for the war in the Pacific. Tellingly, the last exhibition held at the hall in the first months of

1943 was titled the Holy War's Masterpieces of Art, which **showcased** works by officially approved 'war artists' like Fujita Tsuguharu and Miyamoto Saburō.

By the time the Second World War entered its final stages, the exhibition hall had already closed its doors. Fully geared to war production, the city simply did not have the resources to stage any exhibitions, even those meant to drive its impoverished citizens on to greater sacrifices. The last few years of its life, its upper and lower floors

housed a civil engineering branch office for the Chūgoku and Shikoku regions.

At 8:15 a.m. on 6 August 1945, the atomic bomb Little Boy detonated some 600 yards above the roof of the building after a fall of 44.4 seconds from the bomb hatch of Colonel Paul Warfield Tibbets Jr's *Enola Gay*. Along with the building's occupants, some 69.000 of Nagasaki's citizens died in the initial blast. The rest of the total of 140.000 died over the next days, weeks, and months. The

HIROSHIMA – Genbaku Dōmu

city's downtown area, much of it made of wooden structures, was razed to the ground, including all the structures of Hiroshima's beautiful castle. Only a few steel-and-concrete structures, among them the Prefectural Industrial Promotion Hall, remained standing, but only in part. It was largely because the bomb detonated almost exactly overhead that the building's vertical columns were able to withstand the pressure of the 15-kiloton blast.

In less than a split second, the hall went from being an institute of war propaganda to a symbol of war's folly. Initially, the authorities planned to tear down the remaining walls, but there was public resistance and somehow the ruins remained standing while the brave new city began to rise around it. Being the closest remaining structure to the bomb's hypocenter, it was only natural that it was incorporated into the overall design of the Peace Memorial Park, which is largely situated on the northern tip of the elongated island situated between the Hon and Motoyasu rivers. Yet it was only in 1966 that Hiroshima's City Council finally adopted a resolution to permanently preserve what is now known in Japan as the Genbaku Dōmu, or the Atomic Bomb Dome. It was the dome-like metal structure that supported the hall's once copper-

sheeted, domed central roof that gave the structure its new name, a name that will forever be associated with the world's first victims of the devastating effects of an atomic bomb.

Aoi-bashi

When the *Enola Gay*'s bombardier Major Thomas Ferebee honed in on his target he trained his bombsight not on the dome of the Industrial Promotion Hall but on the nearby Aoi Bridge. The reason why the historic bridge was such a perfect target was its shape. Spanning the Hon River at the tip of the peninsula that now harbors the Peace Memorial Park, it had a side arm connecting it to the peninsula, which from above made it look like a huge T: the T for Target.

It was not always so. In a 1644 map of the castle town, the only connection between the island and the rest of the castle town is two bridges, named Hon-*bashi* and Motoyasu-*bashi* after the rivers they

北

crossed at the island's northern tip. The area inside the island is designated at *samurai-machi*, or 'samurai township,' as is most of the area around the vast castle grounds, which in those days extended right up to the east bank of the Hon River. These areas were populated by *buke-yashiki*, the luxurious 'warrior mansions,' of his lordship's many retainers.

The bridge across this section of the Hon River was an important connection, for it was across this bridge that Honshū's main traffic artery, the Saigoku Kaidō passed through the castle town. Before the castle was built during the early 1590s, the high road ran well north of what was then still called Gokamura or the Five Villages, a rudimentary fishing settlement occupying a cluster of islands in the estuary of the Ōta River. Aware that the economic viability of his castle town to be would depend on a good infrastructure, the castle's founder, Mōri Terumoto (1553–1625), wisely decided to redirect the high road to run south of the newly rising castle, straight through the heart of the surrounding castle town. This also ensured a good connection to the important traffic arteries of the Inland Sea. In doing so, he created one of the town's most bustling avenues, known as Hon-*dōri*, which today is a largely roofed pedestrian shopping mall.

It was only after the Edo period, when the Hon River lost its function as Hiroshima Castle's westernmost defense, that a group of wealthy town merchants took up the plan to build a V-shaped wooden bridge at the very tip of the Nakajima Township, the northern part of the island between the Hon and Motoyasu rivers. To finance its construction, a toll fee was levied on all who crossed it, earning the bridge its initial name of Zenitori-*bashi*, or Coin Collecting Bridge. When exactly the

bridge received its current name is unclear, though it was probably somewhere after 1894, when ownership of the bridge was transferred to the municipality and toll fees were no longer levied.

The newly christened Aoi Bridge was swept away on 24 April 1904, when the Ōta River burst its banks in the wake of a torrential rain. It was replaced in 1912 by another **wooden V-shaped footbridge** with wooden girders. Another bridge, the Densha-*bashi*, or **Railway Bridge**, a narrow structure with cast iron girders, stood just a few dozen yards upstream. It carried the tracks of Nagasaki's new Hiroden Streetcar Line, which ran between Hiroshima's central station and the end station of Hiroden on the west bank of the Honda River. The line had a substation at what is now called Genbaku Dōmu-mae, but was then still called Yagura no Shita, which means 'below the turret.' Sadly, the one surviving photograph of both bridges from that era is taken toward the west so

it is not possible to ascertain whether, at that point in time, the huge gate that gave access to the southern end of the castle's west bailey still graced the Hon River's east embankment. In all likelihood, it had already been dismantled for it was around

this time that the castle's southern moat was filled in to accommodate the streetcar line.

The two bridges had straddled the Hon River for just over a decade when, on 5 July 1919, both were severely damaged by another flood that inundated more than three thousand homes and killed seventeen. Both bridges were duly restored but soon after the city council adopted plans to bring the Densha-*bashi* into the 20th century, wide enough to accommodate the city's steadily increasing car traffic and strong enough to support the double tracks of a revamped, two-way street car line. Work on the new bridge made of steel plate was begun in 1932. It was completed two years later at a cost of ¥270.000, which would now amount to roughly $4 million. The new setup resulted in a uniquely H-shaped constellation in that the bridge had a perpendicular side arm by which it was connected to the Aoi-*bashi* at the tip of the island. This essentially made the old footbridge obsolete, and it was decided to dismantle the structure.

Looking southward down Rijō-dōri
from the Hon-dōri intersection

丸三証券
キョーリツ
スクールユニフォーム
エミナル
エミナル
広島 四川飯店
2F
キョーリツ
スクール
ユニフォーム
スクールユニフォーム呉、小ゴーナー開店中！
商工中金
P
P

For four more years Nagasaki's citizens could enjoy walking across the wooden deck of the Aoi-

bashi but in 1938 the bridge was dismantled and its name was transferred to the main bridge. The side-bridge to the Nakajima Township at the tip of the island, however, was left in place. Thus it was that the Aoi Bridge on which bombardier Ferebee trained his sight of that fateful morning in 1945 had the vivid T-shape that had been captured on the aerial photograph just a few weeks earlier.

Though heavily damaged the Aoi Bridge withstood the nuclear blast. Given that it was one of the city's major bridges in one of the region's major traffic arteries, work was immediately begun to restore the bridge. Its reconstruction became part of the wider plan to create a Peace Memorial Park that covered the northern tip of the island and included the ruins of the Product Exhibition Hall. Its guard rails and pillars were finished in the same Aji granite as the park's huge cenotaph to the memory of the atomic bomb victims, causing the projected costs to spiral out of control to ¥5.3 million. At just $1.2 million in today's money, it would not seem much, but in the impoverished post-war

HIROSHIMA – Aoi-bashi

Left The new, ferro-cement Aoi Bridge, with in the background the Product Exhibition Hall. Here the old namesake has already been dismantled

Below: Looking westward across the severely damaged Aoi Bridge. Just how huge the impact of the atomic blast on the bridge deck must have been is borne out by the railway tracks above the bridge's western abutment. The bridge's vehement hinging caused them to be pushed right out of their rebates and remain bent as a silent witness to the titanic forces to which the bridge was exposed

years when resources were in short supply, it was still a lot.

By the early seventies, as Japan was booming again and traffic over the bridge reached new heights, the bridge that had survived the direct impact of a nuclear blast was reverently dismantled and replaced with an even wider bridge to accommodate the double railway tracks as well as two three-lane traffic sections. The new Aoi Bridge, which like its predecessor, has a perpendicular side arm to connect it to the Peace Memorial Park, was completed in 1983 at a total cost of ¥4.8 billion, which equates to roughly $45 million in today's money.

TOMONOURA

The small port of Tomonoura on the northern shore
of the Inland Sea has a history that is as old as (and
probably even older than) Japan's written records.
Its beauty is the subject of several poems in the
Manyōshū, the *Anthology of Ten Thousands
Leaves*, Japan's oldest collection of *waka* poetry,
which was compiled in 759. Nestled in a curved
bay at the eastern head of the Numakuna
Peninsula, the port was a major node in the Inland
Sea's maritime traffic arteries and thus a port of
call for all those who moved between Japan's central and western regions.

Enpuku-ji

The Enpuku-*ji*, a Shingon sect temple that is linked
to a small temple that originally stood on the
grounds of the Nunakuma Shrine on the northwest
outskirts of the port, has a far shorter history. It was
founded only in the early Edo period, when the
temple building was moved to the prominent headland that flanks the port's curved inlet on the east.
Formerly, the headland used to be a small island
that housed a castle that controlled the port's maritime traffic, but with the construction of a new
castle on a hill overlooking the port from the north,
the island was connected to the mainland to
improve the harbor's protection from the elements.

The temple grounds' former military purpose is still in evidence in a photograph from 1927, in which one can see the white raised parapet atop the stacked stone walls that can be seen in so many surviving castles around Japan.

When the Japanese photographer Kusakabe Kimbei visited the port by ship half a century earlier, he must have climbed its mast to get the photograph of the Enpuku Temple he did, for it is clearly taken from the water. Using what would have

TOMONOURA – *Enpuku-ji*

Left: Benten Island, as framed by the open window of the Fukuzen Temple

Right: The Fukuzen Temple in 1927

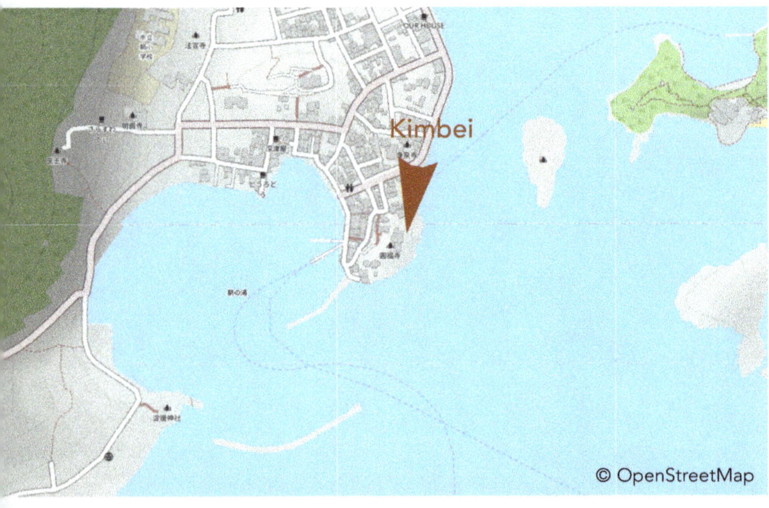

amounted to a zoom lens, Kimbei could also have taken his image from the elevated grounds of the Fukuzen-*ji*, a temple that stands just a stone's throw toward the north from the Enpuku Temple. In those days, the water came right up to the foot of the base on which the latter temple stands, creating the impression one is hovering above the water.

Fukuzen-ji

The Fukuzen Temple is definitely the best place from which to view nearby Benten Island, which lies just to the east of the old port. In the olden days, the island was also known as Hyakkan-*jima*,

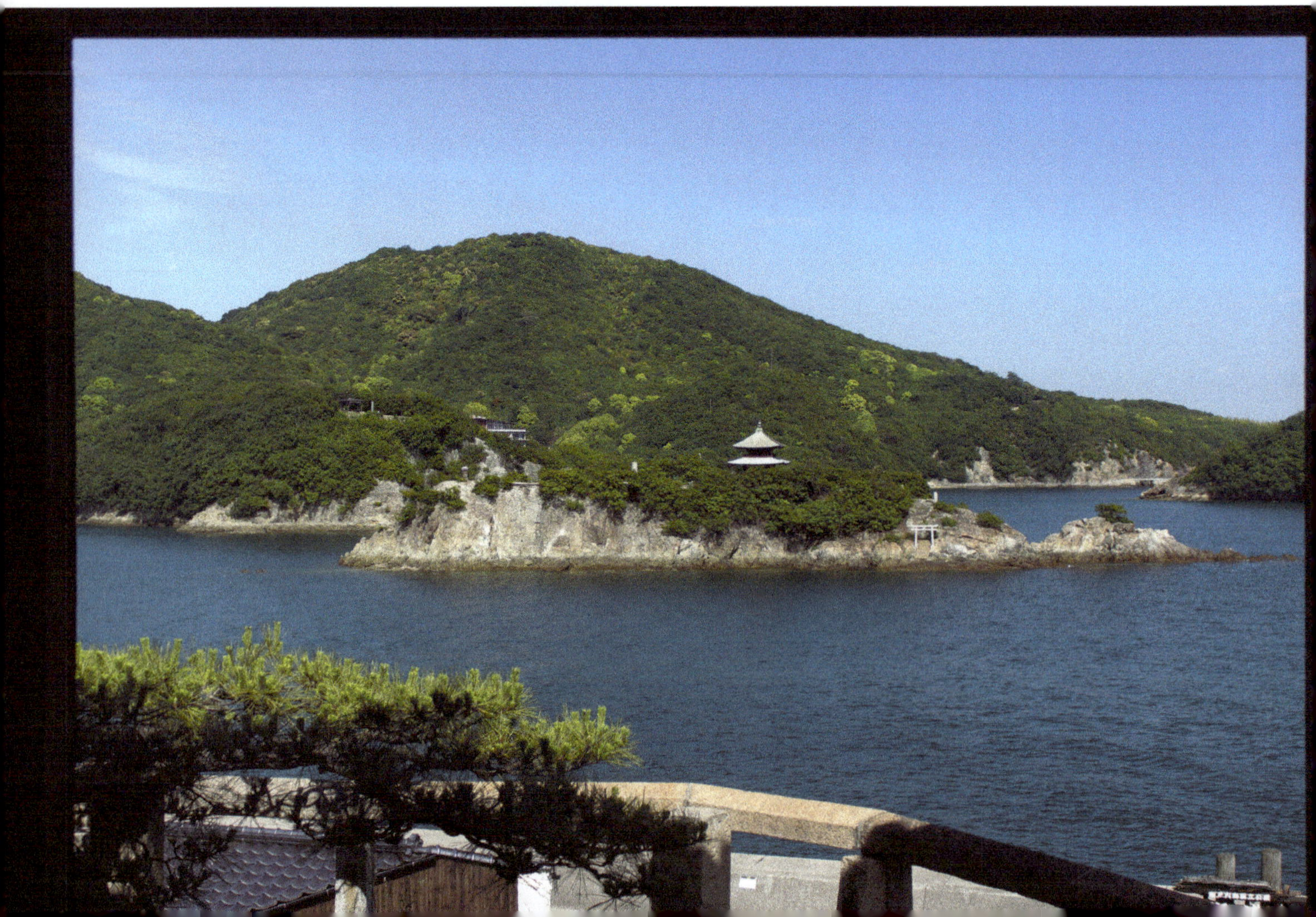

or 'One-Hundred-*kan* Island.' It is said that, during the Muromachi period, a warrior from Ōmi by the name of Fukiwara Masamichi was making his way back from a pilgrimage to the Itsukushima Shrine when, stopping over on the small island for a rest, he dropped his sword in the sea. Eager to recover his treasured weapon, he turned to the local fishermen, promising them a reward of a hundred *kan*—a small fortune—if they managed to retrieve it. The fishermen, afraid of the sharks, refused to enter the water. But when Masamichi began to scold and ridicule them, a young man eager to save their honor, plunged into the water. He retrieved the weapon but was so mauled by a shark that he soon afterward expired. Moved by the courage of the young fisherman, Masamichi used his reward to erect a monument in his honor.

Kusakabe Kimbei (1841–1934) was a native of Kai Province (Yamanashi Prefecture). In his early twenties, he moved to Yokohama, where he found employment as a colorist at Felice Beato's studio, learning the art of photography and developing photographic plates. In 1867, he joined Beato when the latter visited Shanghai. When, in 1877, Beato sold his studio to fellow photographers Raimund von Stillfried and Hermann Andersen, Kimbei stayed on at the studio, until, in 1881, he opened his own studio called Kimbei Shashin on Benten-*dōri*. One of the highlights in his career as a photographer came in 1904, when a number of his works went on display at the Louisiana Purchase Exposition, an international exposition held in St. Louis, Missouri.

Tomonoura today

AKASHI

Akashi-jō

As with so many other Japanese cities, it was a castle that put Akashi on the map. Once, the Akashi territories had been part of the vast domain of Himeji. But in 1617 the *Bakufu* in Edo decided to break the domain up into smaller ones. One of these was the domain of Akashi, which guarded two main traffic arteries: the Chūgoku Kaidō and the Akashi Straits. They appointed Ogasawara Tadazane as its new lord. Tadazane was a staunch Tokugawa supporter, who had fought hard in the siege of Osaka Castle. He had only survived by the breadth of a hair. For months he lay on the brink of death, having sustained severe wounds in as many as seven places. Both his brother and father had died, leaving the leadership of the clan to the 20-year-old.

Only just married, Tadazane and his wife first took up residence at Funage Castle, a small stronghold on the eastern perimeter of the former Himeji domain. It proved to be outdated and far too small for a domain the size of Akashi. And so it was decided that Tadazane and his wife should have a new residence. Still young and inexperienced, Tadazane, whose honorific name was Ukon no Taifu, called in the help of his neighbor and father-in-law, Honda Mino no Kami, alias, Honda Tadamasa, the lord of Himeji Castle. The *Honda kaki*, the old records of the Honda clan describes how:

> During the summer, the *bakufu* issued a decree to build a new castle at Akashi, and master Lord Honda Mino no Kami and Master Ukon con-

sulted with the *shōgun* on the matter. And in order to give a good account of its geographical features, his lordship visited Akashi several times to inspect locations at an inlet along the seashore in the vicinity of Shioya, at a rising ground called Kamakazaka just west of Akashi, and at Hitomaru-*yama* in Akashi. And after further consultation, it was decided that Akashi Castle should be built at Hitomaru-*yama*.

One of the reasons why Hitomaru-*yama* was chosen was the presence of a large lake, which was expanded to serve as a moat for the castle's defense. Work was begun early in 1619 and carried out on a grand scale. Thousands of laborers were put to work on its construction, while a small army of architects, designers, and military specialists was employed to manage the huge undertaking.

One of the many specialists consulted in the construction of Akashi Castle was the legendary swordsman and military strategist Miyamoto Musashi. He was appointed extraordinary advisor to the *zōei bugyō*, the construction magistrate in charge of the project, helping with the layout of the castle town, the construction of the castle walls, as well as a harbor and its defenses. Yet Musashi was not only consulted on military matters. The *Seiryūwa*, the private writings of the Ogasawara clan, describe how, following the completion of the castle's main structures, the young lord began work on embellishing the new home for himself and his wife:

> Facing the west side of the third bailey of Akashi Castle was a narrow strip of enclosed land stretching northward. On the part that was

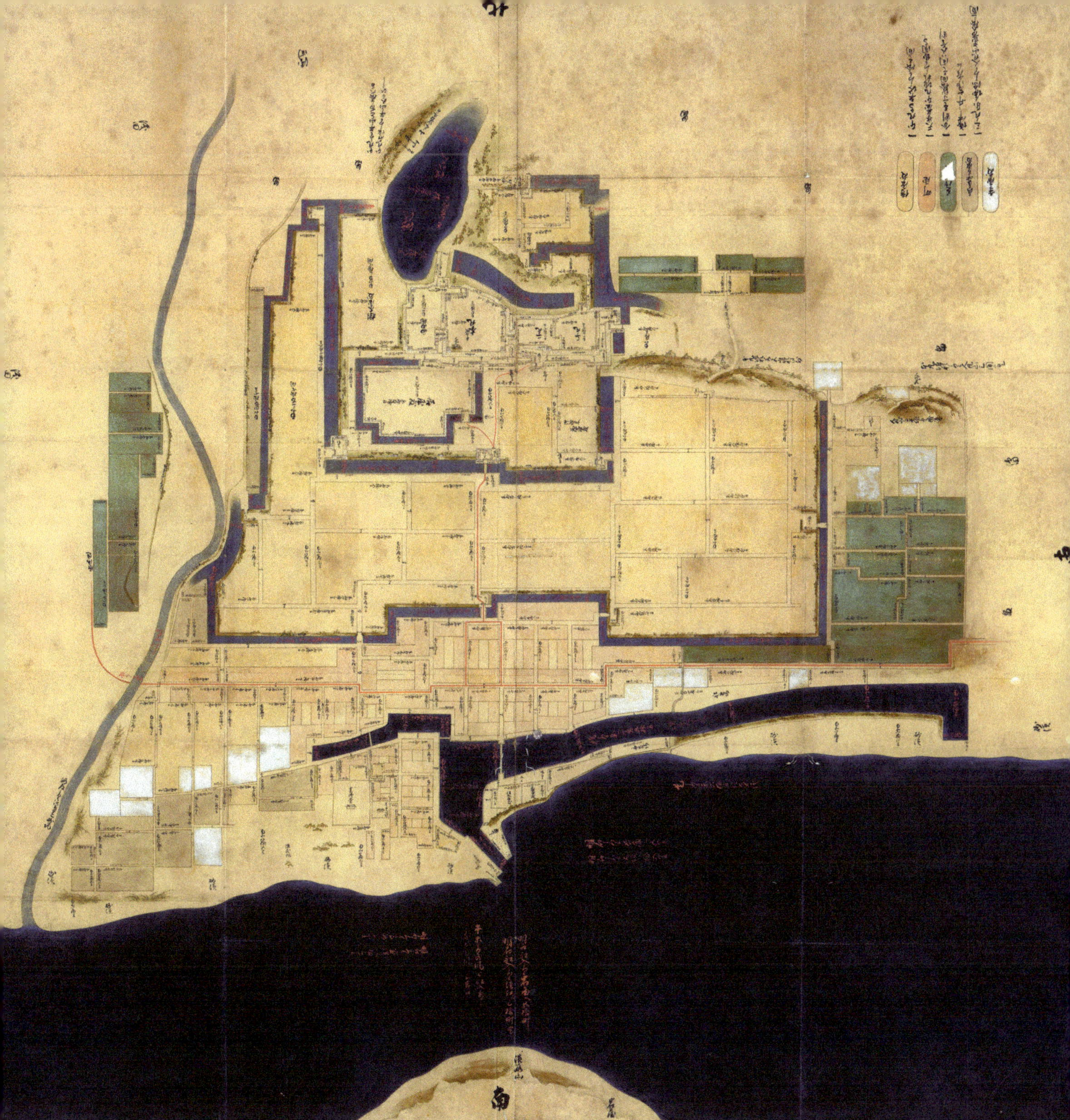

barren and uninhabited, his lordship built a *yashiki* surrounded with trees and shrubs, so it could be used as an area for recreation and the performance of tea ceremonies, and in addition to this, a public bath with adjacent *tatami* rooms, and a field for playing ball. He put Miyamoto Musashi in charge of the construction of the tea house, miniature mountains, a miniature lake, and a waterfall, as well as the planting of trees and shrubs.

AKASHI – Akashi-jō

Below: Akashi Castle during the early Meji period, when the castle grounds had already been turned into a municipal park

Right: Akashi Castle today, still a worthy subject for a painting

Much of the material for the castle was harvested from smaller local castles that were demolished: Funage, Miki, Takasago, Edayoshi. Thus its central southeast turret, the Tatsumi-*yagura* was taken from Funage Castle. Its southwest turret, the Hitsujisaru-*yagura*, came from farther afield, all the way from Fushimi Castle. All the way from Nakatsu on the southern island of Kyushu came a whole keep. Yet even though its foundations were laid and are still there to this day, it was never actually placed. Instead, its materials were redirected to other parts of the castle.

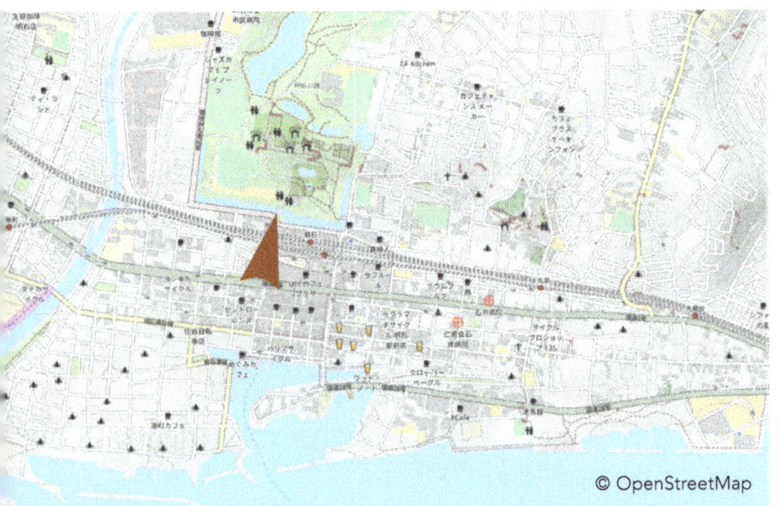

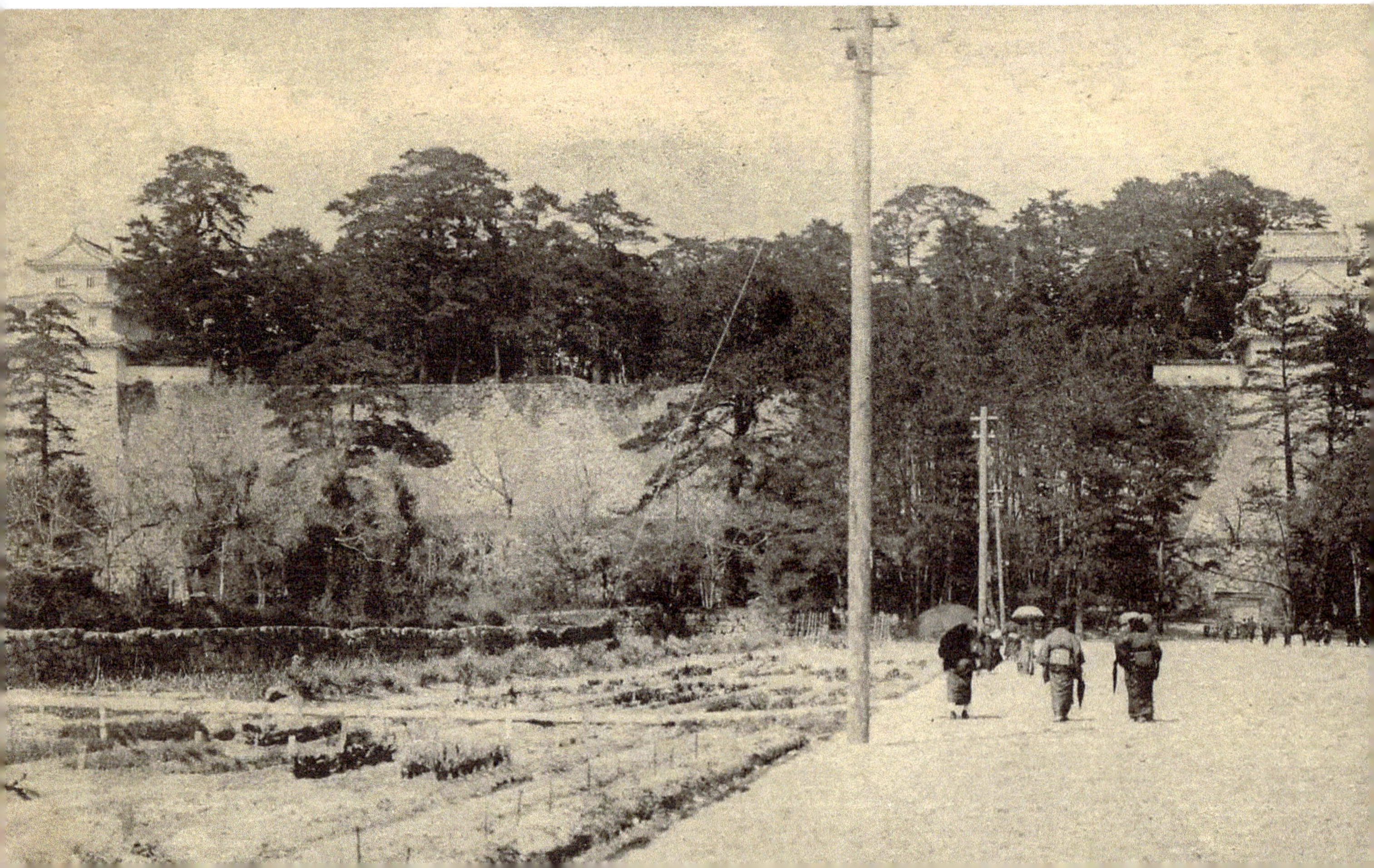

For two and a half centuries, Akashi Castle guarded traffic along the Chūgoku Kaidō and through the Akashi Straits, until 1873, when it was no longer needed and listed for demolition by the new Meiji government. In 1881 its eastern turret was dismantled to provide material for the building of a

high school, but two years later, the remains of the castle walls and the castle grounds, which had been maintained by local voluntaries, was turned into a municipal park. In 1901, restoration was begun on the Tatsumi-*yagura* and the Hitsujisaru-*yagura*, the Southeast Turret and the Southwest Turret, though the northern turret was dismantled. The inner and outer citadels, which were in poor repair, were likewise demolished, as was the **Ōte-mon**, the old main gate. As elsewhere, only the castle's inner citadel was preserved for posterity. Its outer baileys were dismantled to make way for the expanding city.

Kinkō-bashi

Faint outlines of the castle's former outer baileys can still be traced in Akashi's present-day city plan. One of these is the wide avenue that ran south from the castle's central Taiko Gate. Today, it has to pass under the elevated tracks of the Sanyō Densha and JR railway lines, as well as the National Route No. 2. In the old days, the avenue terminated at a narrow wooden footbridge that connected

the castle town to a sliver of land abreast Akashi's bustling port. Called Nakasaki Island, it was the playground of the lords of Akashi Castle, who would come down to the island in their spare time

to enjoy the stunning view toward Awaji Island whilst enjoying a cup of tea at the domain's *chaya*, or 'tea house.' The bridge, at that time, was known

as the Chaya-*bashi*. Besides the tea house, the island also was home to the domain's granaries, boathouses, and the dwellings of those who manned the Akashi fleet.

During the early Meiji period, when the castle was decommissioned and its buildings lost their function, they were turned to other purposes. Some of the dwellings on the island were converted into brothels. The bridge, which was rebuilt several times during its lifespan, was renamed Daikoku-*bashi*. In 1911, to accommodate the growing use of cars, the narrow footbridge was replaced by a wide earth and stone bridge with a short wooden section to enable the passage of the small boats with which the local fishermen fished for oysters and set out eel traps. It was renamed Kinkō-*bashi*, or 'Brocade Inlet Bridge' to celebrate the beauty of the area.

After the war, the destroyed Kinkō-*bashi* was replaced by a concrete bridge, which straddles the harbor a few hundred feet eastward from where

AKASHI – Kinkō-bashi

the old bridge stood. Much of Nakajima Island, too, has disappeared, its eastern part having been swallowed up in the wave of land-reclamation that characterized Japan's post-war period.

Gankirō

One of the brothels on Nakasaki Island was known as the **Gankirō**. The wooden two-story building displayed all the craftsmanship of Japan's feudal artisans. It had the wide latticed downstairs windows that flanked a central entranceway shaded by a richly decorated gable roof. Over it sat a second story with stuccoed walls surrounded by a wide veranda, which in turn was crowned by a beautiful hip-and-gable roof. The typical Edo-period structure managed to survive right into the 21st century, until the summer of 2016, that is, when it was surrounded by scaffolding with tarpaulins and quietly dismantled. It seems the wealthy occupants

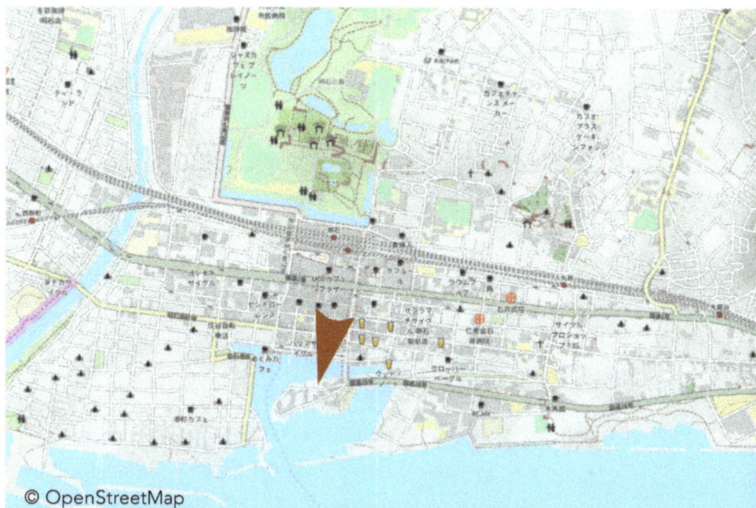

of Akashi's prestigious sea-side residences preferred not to be reminded of their area's colorful history.

Maiko no Hama

One thing that made Maiko no Hama, or Maiko Beach (some 5 km east of Akashi) such an attractive place during the Edo period was that it sat along the Akashi-*kaikyō*, the narrow straits that separates the main island of Honshu from that of Awaji, which lies across the eastern section of the Inland Sea. Being the main gateway to the commercial hub of Osaka, the straits in those days were navigated by hundreds of *bezai-sen*, round-hulled and carvel-planked (overlapping planks) vessel with junk-type rigging. They were also known as *kitamae-bune* or 'north-bound ships,' for they would round the long island of Honshu through the Straits of Shimonoseki and sail all the way up to the northern port of Ishikari in far-away Hokkaidō (then still called Ezo).

The Akashi Straits are still one of Japan's busiest traffic lanes, with more than a thousand vessels passing through it every day. Not only maritime traffic is intense. Every day, more than thirty thousand vehicles cross the Akashi Kaikyō Ōhashi, the huge suspension bridge that straddles the Akashi Straits and, together with the Ōnaruto and Konaruto bridges, connects the mainland of Honshū to the island of Awaji and, on the other side of the island, to the island of Shikoku. When it was completed in 1998, it had the longest central span in the world at 6,532 feet; now, it is still a close second after the Çanakkale Bridge across the Dardanelles Straits in Turkey.

The soothing white sands that used to line the shoreline at Maiko no Hama have long since gone. They have been replaced by the concrete promenade of the Maiko Higashi Seaside Park, from where one can marvel at the engineering feat of the Akashi Kaikyō Ōhashi.

KOBE

Kyoryūchi

Like Yokohama, Kobe's architecture during the late 19th century was heavily influenced by international politics. Under the Treaty of Amity and Commerce between the United States and Japan of 1858, the nearby port of Hyōgo was to be opened to foreign vessels in 1863. It eventually took until 1868 before foreign vessels could freely enter the harbor, though it was not the port of Hyōgo, but the newly created port of Kobe. Hyōgo, after all, was already a very busy domestic port, and keeping the foreigners away from densely populated areas would help prevent any clashes with the locals.

Foreign ships brought foreign traders. To house them, the Japanese authorities conceded a stretch

of land in front of the port to the foreign powers with which the treaties were signed. The area was known as Kobe's *kyoryūchi* or 'foreign settlement.' Measuring 25 hectares, its borders were demarcated by the Koi River to the west, the Saigoku Kaidō to the north, and the Ikuta River to the east.

Building within the area only started slowly. Japan, during the last two years of the 1860s, was in the throes of a civil war, and while the area's administration was technically governed by its extraterritorial status, the rapidly changing situation on the ground meant that until the end of the

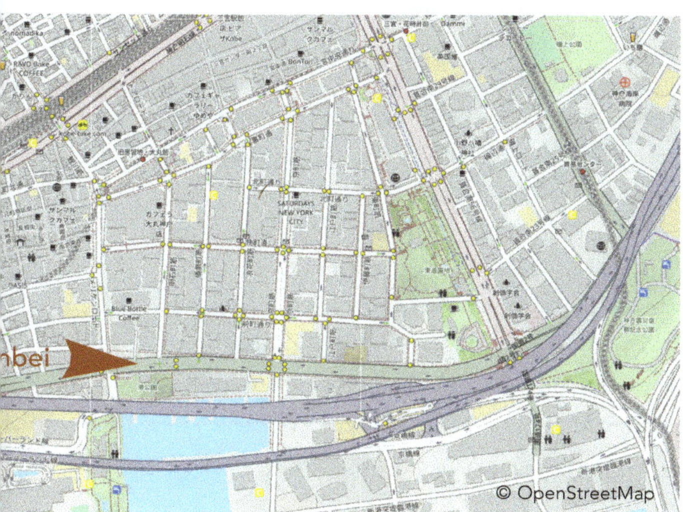

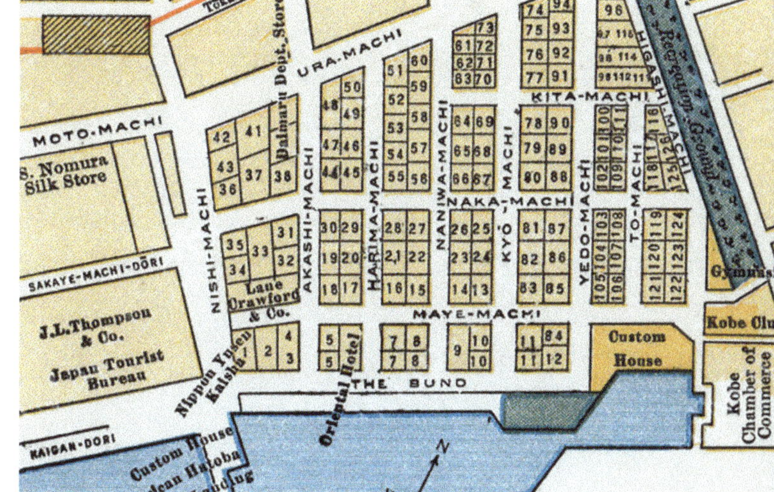

Boshin War, the port only had a customs house and a few storehouses. Things improved with the establishment of the Meiji government. Though it refused foreigners to own land within the settle-ments, it did allow them to perpetually lease it. All bidding had been concluded by the beginning of 1873, and by the end of the decade much of the leased area had been developed. The port grew so fast that within two decades its population had grown from a few thousand to more than a hundred thousand.

The layout of the foreign settlement was straight-forward: a checkered grid of building blocks sep-arated by wide streets. Unlike regular Japanese cities in which city blocks have numbers, Kobe's streets had names (Edo-*machi*, Harima-*machi*, Sakae-*machi*, etc.). The settlement's main avenue was the Kaigan-*dōri*, or the 'Coast Street,' better known as The Bund by the port's foreign settlers. In front of it, four new wharves were built, while the Ikuta River was redirected to keep the harbor from silting up.

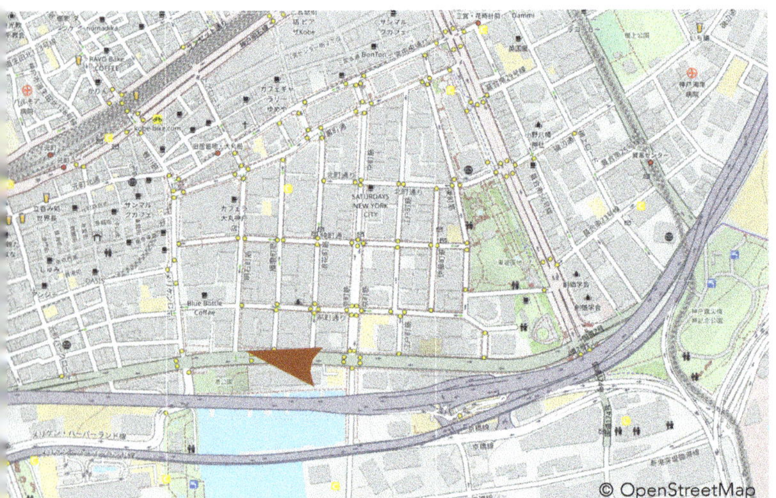

Left: Looking westward along The Bund today, with, toward the right, the Mitsui and Osaka Merchant Shipping buildings, and, in the distance, the old Post Office building

Below: The ffully restored former American consulate today

The foreign settlement underwent great changes during the early 20th century, after the Japanese had managed to negotiate the return of the foreign settlements. Now, Japanese companies like Mitsui and Osaka Merchant Shipping were able to open their offices on The Bund in large buildings designed by prestigious architects like Alexander Nelson Hansell (1857–1940).

Many of the foreign settlement's historic buildings were lost again in the massive air raids of the Second World War. Some that did survive the air raids, were lost half a century later, when the Kobe area was struck by an earthquake with a magnitude of 7.3 (its epicenter lay at the northern tip of Awaji

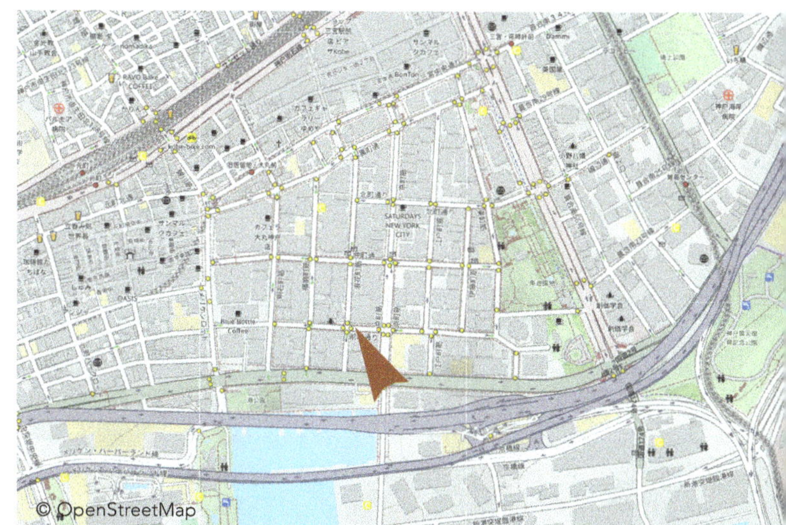

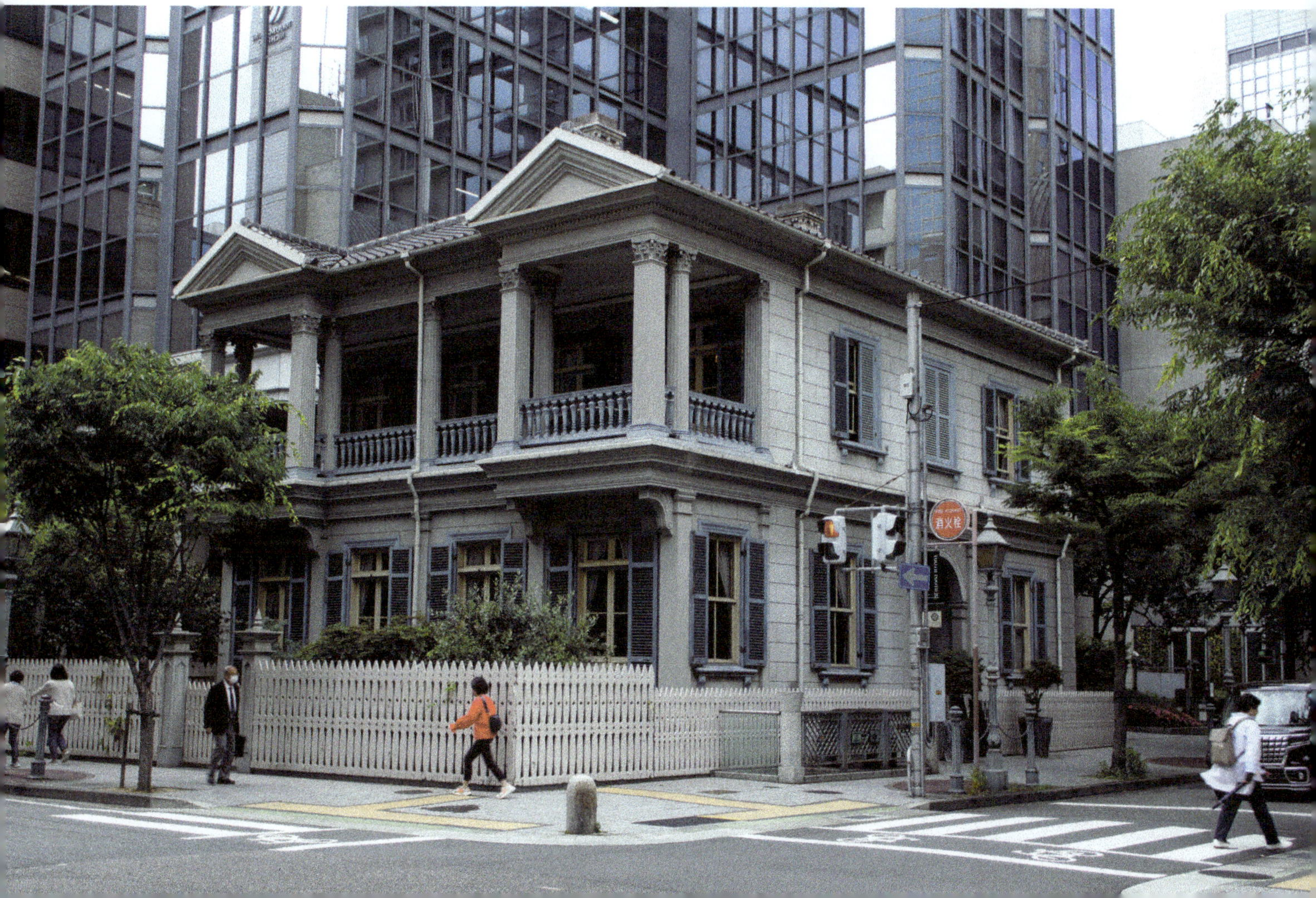

Island). One of its casualties was the former American consulate building, which had graced the corner of Kyō-*machi* and Mae-*machi* for more than a century. A two-floored brick and wood building adorned with pediments and classical columns, it epitomized the atmosphere of the late 19th-century foreign settlement. Being the sole surviving structure in Kobe from this era, it had been designated an Important Cultural Property in 1989. A year later, the building underwent extensive repairs and restoration work and was reopened as a restau-

rant, only to be **flattened by the earthquake** five years later. Not all of the building's materials, however, were lost. This, combined with the building's historic value, caused the local, regional, and central authorities to chip in, and not long after the rubble was cleared and sorted work was started to restore the building to its original glory. In the end, some 70% of its original materials were reused to create an exact copy of the original, though this time using cutting-edge technology to make the structure earthquake-proof.

Oriental Hotel

One of the foreign settlement's most historic buildings was the Oriental Hotel. Next to Nagasaki's Hotel Belle Vue, it was one of the first Western-style hotels. It opened its doors in 1870 and would remain in business until the Great Hanshin earthquake of 1995. During its century-long lifespan, the hotel went through a number of iterations. The **first hotel** was opened at number 79 Kyō-*machi* Avenue. Its founder and first proprietor seems to have been a man by the name of Gerardus van

der Vlies, a former Dutch naval physician who had settled in Kobe during the 1860s.

In 1886, the hotel was acquired by the French chef Louis Begeux, who, together with his wife, ran a restaurant called Restaurant Francaise at number 122, opposite Kobe's custom house. Begeux moved the hotel to number 81, one block closer to the seaside. It seems that Begeux's talents in the kitchen surpassed those of his competitors. Or perhaps his dishes were just better appreciated by Western visitors who preferred a taste of home over the local fare. One foreigner who stayed at the new Kobe's Oriental Hotel was the British author Rudyard Kipling. Kipling had been traveling through India, Burma, and China, and was now doing Japan, an experience he recorded in his travel memoir, *From Sea to Sea and Other Sketches, Letters of Travel*. He had crossed over from Hong Kong to Nagasaki in the fall of 1889 and reached Kobe by way of the Inland Sea. From there, he intended to travel over land toward Kyoto, Nagoya, and Yokohama, to take a boat to San Francisco:

Yet, ere I go further, let me sing the praises of the excellent M. Begeux, proprietor of the Oriental Hotel, upon whom be peace. His is a house where you can dine. He does not merely feed you. His coffee is the coffee of the beautiful France. For tea he gives you Peliti cakes (but better) and the *vin ordinaire* which is *compris*, is good. Excellent Monsieur and Madame Begeux! If the Pioneer were a medium for puffs, I would write a leading article upon your potato salad, your beefsteaks, your fried fish, and your

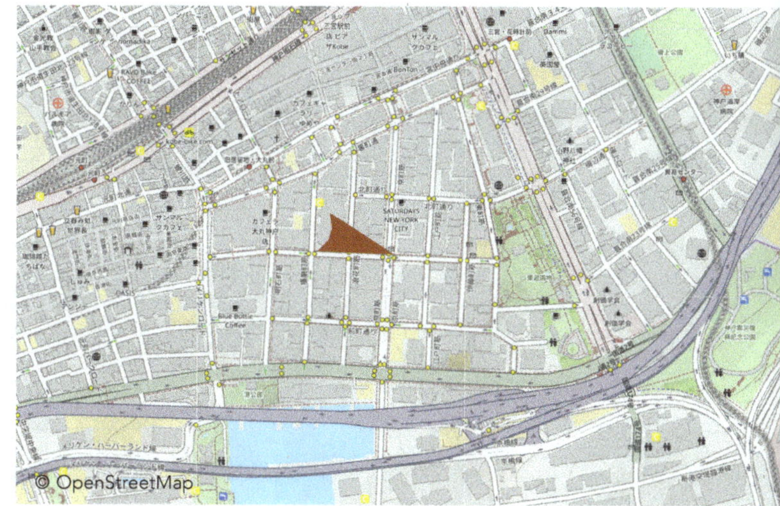

Below: Kobe's new Oriental Hotel at No. 6 along The Bund

Right: Kobe's new Oriental Hotel as seen from the water

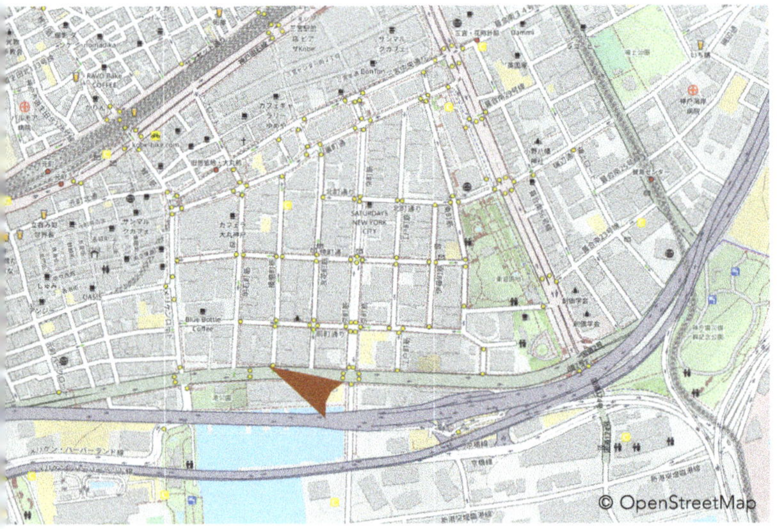

staff of highly trained Japanese servants in blue tights, who looked like so many small Hamlets without the velvet cloak, and who obeyed the unspoken wish. No, it should be a poem—a ballad of good living. I have eaten curries of the rarest at the Oriental at Penang, the turtle steaks of Raffles's at Singapur still live in my regretful memory, and they gave me chicken liver and sucking-pig in the Victoria at Hong Kong which I will always extol. But the Oriental at Kobe was better than all three. Remember this, and so shall you who come after slide round a quarter of the world upon a sleek and contented stomach.

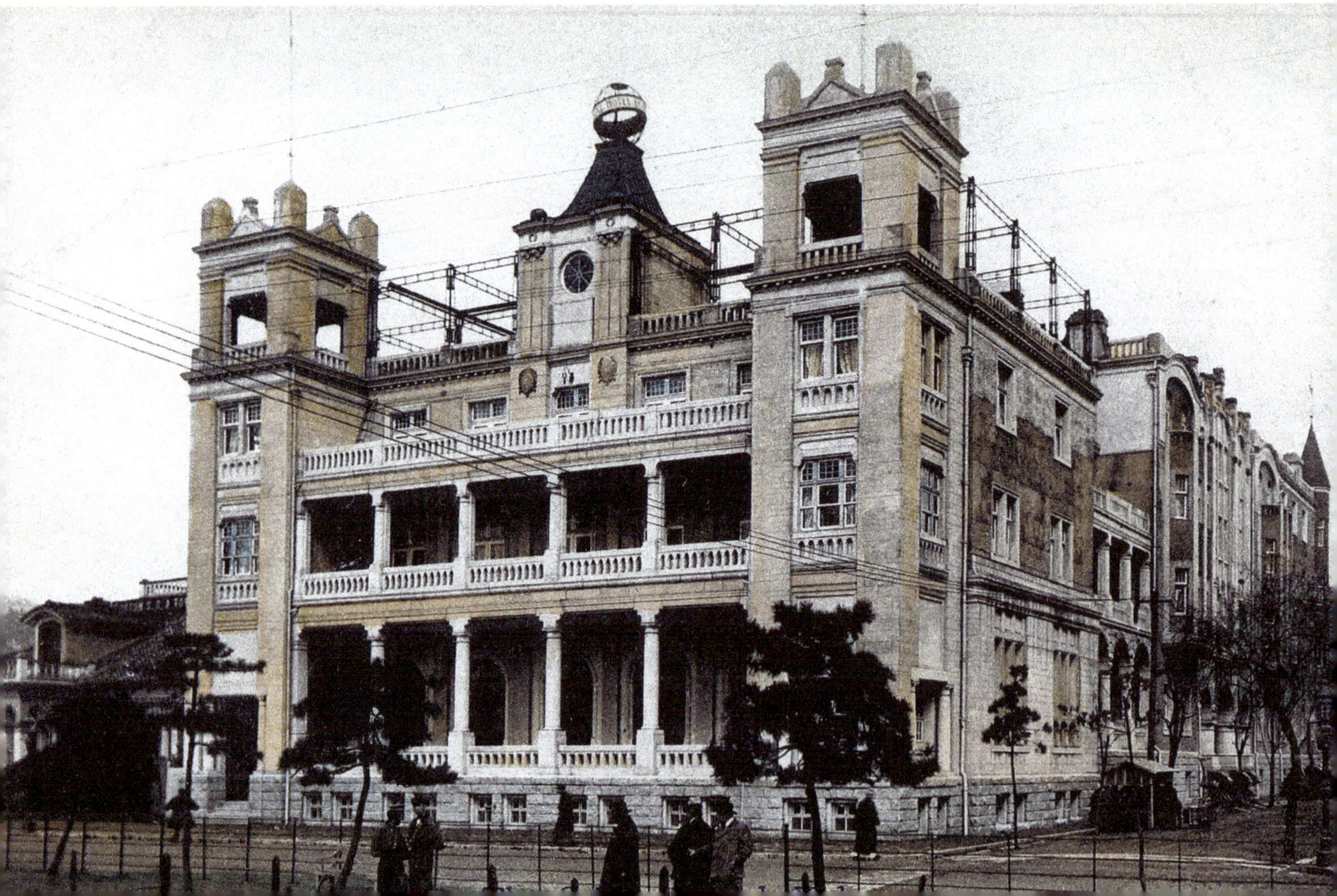

The third iteration of Kobe's Oriental Hotel saw the light when a group of foreign businessmen led by Arthur Hasketh Groom and Edward Hazlett purchased it in 1897. They made the hotel a limited company and hired its French chef as its manager. The new business venture went so well that, in 1907, the hotel was moved yet again, this time to number 6, facing the Inland Sea across The Bund. They hired the prestigious Yokohama-based construction company of Georg de Lalande. Its chief architect was Jan Letzel, the Czech architect who went on to design Hiroshima's Prefecture's Product Exhibition Hall (see page 33). Letzel, who had only just arrived in Japan, was the son of hotel owners in Bohemia, and was the perfect candidate to build a Western-style hotel in Kobe.

The resulting structure had all the trappings of a European hotel from the turn of the century. Its main façade was set back between two rectangular towers, with wide balconies connecting the two. Erected out of stone, hard plaster, and concrete, its architectural style was bold with only simple ornamentations—just some dentils on the soffit and sober but decorative balustrades along the balconies. As such, it reflected the work of Letzel's teacher and compatriot Jan Kotera (1871–1923), and the Austrian architect Otto Wagner, both exponents of the Baroque Vienna Secessionists, a movement closely related to Art Nouveau.

The hotel's restaurant menu, too, was bold, at least by Japanese standards, as it featured the now highly prized Kobe beef. During the Edo period, the Japanese shunned the eating of meat of cows (along with most other livestock animals). But during the early Meiji period, farmers north of Kobe,

a group of Japanese businessmen who established the Oriental Hotel Ltd.

For almost four decades Kobe's Oriental Hotel entertained the Japanese and foreign well-to-do at number 6. One of them was the Japanese novelist Tanizaki Junichirō. A native of Tokyo, Junichirō moved to Kobe in 1928 and was charmed by the hotel's cosmopolitan atmosphere. Enough, at any rate, to make it a meeting place for the characters that populate *The Makioka Sisters*, his novel about a wealthy Osaka upper-middle-class family.

who had been rearing cattle for use on farms and in oxcarts, began to do so to meet the growing demand for meat by Kobe's expat community.

In 1917, the hotel was bought by the Toyo Kisen Shipping Line. Its interiors were **completely refurbished** to accommodate the shipping line's international passengers. To increase the hotel's capacity, a fourth story was added, swallowing up the corner towers and the frontal balconies and causing it to lose much of its 'oriental' charm. Nine years later, the hotel was sold again, this time to

The world described so well by Junichirō was swept away during the last months of the Second World War, when Kobe became the target of a total of 128 Allied air raids. The largest raid came on the night of 16 to 17 March 1945, when 331 B-29 Superfortresses released a total of more than 2000 tons of incendiary and fragmentation bombs over the industrial but also densely populated urban area. The result was commensurate: 20% of the city was destroyed in the resulting firestorm, including five hundred factories and the vast

Kawasaki shipyards. By the end of the war, some ten thousand of Kobe's citizens had been killed, forty thousand wounded, and close to half a million left homeless. More than half of the city's urban area had gone up in flames and more than a hundred thousand buildings had been destroyed or damaged. Among them was the Oriental Hotel, which was struck in an air raid on 5 June.

Badly damaged, the Oriental Hotel was partially restored. A new annex was added to the rear of the old hotel, but it was cheaply done and the restored building reflected the impoverished post-war years. It seems that during this interlude, the hotel did not accommodate any overnight guests but mainly served as a banqueting hall with a grill and a diner.

In 1964, a new, fourth iteration, opened its doors. It was the year of the Olympic Games, and over the previous years, riding the wave of an economic upsurge, the whole country had been brimming

with a huge number of prestigious construction projects, the most impressive being the Tōkaidō Shinkansen. In Kobe, it was the new Oriental Hotel that set the tone of the city's post-war revival. Raised in chocolate-brown marble, the new structure was in keeping with the times. It was also Japan's first (and thus far only) hotel to sport a small lighthouse atop its roof, just behind a dining area with a panoramic view of the harbor. The elevated position was necessary because the hotel had lost its coveted location along The Bund. The

new structure was situated at number 25-26 Naka-*machi*, just across the road from where the original hotel had started out almost a century earlier.

For exactly two decades the new Oriental Hotel catered to Japan's growing affluent class, as well as visiting foreigners, among them a string of celebrities that included actress Marilyn Monroe, baseball giant Joe DiMaggio, activist Helen Keller, and James-Bond-actor Sean Connery when filming You Only Live Twice in Kobe's dockyards with his love-interest played by Akiko Wakabayashi.

Disaster struck in the early morning of 17 January 1995, when Kobe was hit by the **Great Hanshin earthquake**. The Oriental Hotel survived the tremors, which lasted for almost half a minute. But like so many other of the city's buildings, its structure was too badly damaged for the hotel to reopen. For almost a decade the building stood empty, until it was eventually dismantled.

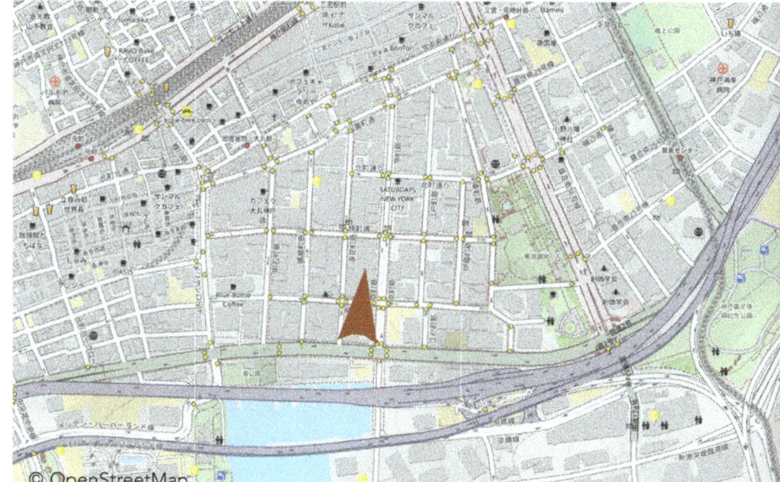

Soon enough, however, plans were hatched to build a new Oriental Hotel. In 2006 its premises at number 25 were acquired by Mitsui Fudōsan. The public company Plan · Do · See, which was to operate the new hotel, even acquired the trademark rights from the Daiei supermarket chain, which had owned the former hotel. Two years later, work was begun on a new, 17-story hotel with 100 guest rooms and 5 banqueting halls. Work was completed in the spring of 2010, when the Oriental Hotel Kobe opened its doors.

By then, however, the distinction of being Kobe's 'oriental' hotel had become somewhat blurred. Already in 1988, Daiei had opened the Shin Kobe Oriental City—combining a 600-room hotel, shopping center, and theatre—on Kobe's northern outskirts. Their most prestigious project in Kobe came to fruition in 1995, when the futuristic-looking Meriken Park Oriental Hotel went into business. Situated on a pier in front of the city, the hotel caters to the more than a hundred cruise ships that call at the port annually, as they can dock right in front of the hotel. All three hotels make allusions to the old Oriental Hotel in their own way, but none does so convincingly, perhaps out of fear of being branded too old-fashioned. Even the Oriental Hotel Kobe hasn't bothered to use the old hotel's trademark, opting instead for a more ornamental logo, though it still carries a prominent letter 'H.'

Nevertheless, today's Oriental Hotel Kobe can still be considered the rightful successor to the truly 'oriental' hotel built by Jan Letzel. It may no longer have wide balconies for its guest to take in the view of Kobe Bay, but it still attracts foreign guests lured by the hotel's romanticism, for it rightfully 'boasts a history of over 150 years.'

One relic of the former, 4th iteration of the hotel is its old **lighthouse**, which miraculously survived the jolts of the earthquake atop the building. It now sits on the upper deck of the Meriken Park Oriental Hotel, casting its alternating red and green beams over the modern port.

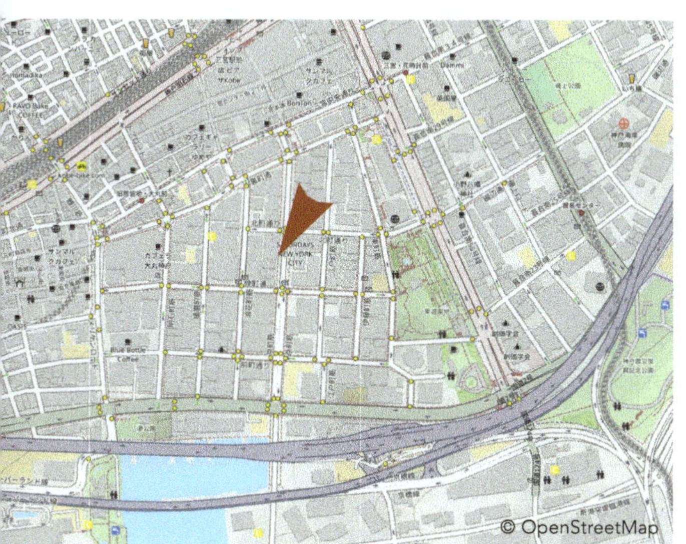

Kobe as seen from the water today, dominated by
the cruise-ship-like Meriken Park Oriental Hotel

Kobe Muslim Masjid

A structure that survived both the Second World War air raids as well as the Great Hanshin earthquake is the **Kobe Muslim Masjid**. Built in 1935, it was Japan's first mosque. Kobe had been the home of a number of Indian and Turkish Muslim

traders since the port had been opened to foreign ships in 1868. They had practiced their religion among themselves in private homes. During the 1920s, they (and a handful of Japanese converts) were joined by Tartar Muslims who had fled Russia in the wake of the October Revolution. By the end of the decade, the number of Muslims in Kobe had grown to a few hundred, and the need for a public place to practice led to the first initiative to build a mosque.

The first plans to build a mosque were drawn up in 192. Permission was granted on 14 November 1934, and the first cornerstone was laid two weeks later. Remarkably, the man who designed the mosque was another Check national, the architect Jan Josef Švagr (1885–1969). A few years earlier,

Švagr had found employment with the Tokyo-based architectural bureau of the Check-born Antonin Raymund (who in turn had come to Japan with Frank Lloyd Wright to work on Tokyo's Imperial Hotel). It was through Raymund that Švagr began to work with concrete, the first such example being

a Catholic mission girl's school in Yokohama.

When the mosque was opened on Friday 2 August 1935, its Muslim parish received a letter of congratulation from Kobe's Mare:

As Mayor of Kobe, I have much pleasure in extending to the Kobe Muslim Mosque Committee my hearty congratulations on the occasion of the opening of the Mosque. It is the first Muslim Mosque built in Japan, and Kobe may well be proud of it. The appearance of the New Mosque is quite befitting such a Cosmopolitan city as Kobe, and it adds a new attraction to the already numerous places of interest in the city.

For ten years, the Kobe Muslim Masjid served as a place of worship for Kobe's Muslim community. By then, its members included citizens from India, China, Manchuria, Russia, Afghanistan, Indonesia, and Egypt. But in 1943, the Imperial Japanese Navy requisitioned the mosque because the concrete structure had a large basement considered bomb-proof. This it certainly was, for post-war photographs show it was one of the few structures to remain standing at the end of the war. In **one of these photographs**, to the right of the mosque in the distance, one can see the two towers of the Nakayamate Catholic Church, which also survived the air raids but not the 1995 earthquake.

After the war, the mosque was again opened for prayer. During the Great Hanshin earthquake, the mosque withstood the tremors and was used as a shelter for those who had lost their homes. Today, the mosque serves the prefecture's more than 5,000-strong Muslim community.

Hanshin Expressway

Another structure to fall prey to the Great Hanshin earthquake of 1984 was the elevated section of the Hanshin Expressway's Kobe Route. More than half of its 1,175 pillars and well over a third of its 1,304 girders sustained serious damage. Due to the vehement sideway jolts, seventeen of the massive supporting pillars snapped like matchsticks, causing a section of some 630 m to collapse sideways onto the eastbound lanes of the ground-level National Route No. 2. Miraculously, only sixteen people—out of a total of 6,434 in greater Kobe— lost their lives on the expressway. This was partly due to the time at which the earthquake struck, it being still only 5:46. Had it struck two hours later, during peak hour, it would have been far worse. Another reason for the low death toll on the expressway was that the collapsed section did not disintegrate but remained largely intact, which

made it possible for some who had been caught on the collapsing section to walk away unhurt.

Suspicions began to circulate in the media that corners had been cut in the expressway's construction. The construction was evidently faulty, but not because of negligence or corruption; it had simply been built to meet the building standards in force at the time of construction, which dated back to 1952. Tellingly, those standards are now known in Japan as the *Kyū-Taishin Kijun*, or the 'Old Earthquake-Proof Standards,' as opposed to the *Shin-Taishin Kijun*, or the 'New Earthquake-Proof Standards,' which date from 1981. Since then, those standards have undergone a number of revisions, each one in response to the deficiencies that have been highlighted by subsequent earthquakes.

Given that the Kobe Route of the Hanshin Expressway carried some 40% of local traffic, work was immediately begun to rebuild the structure to the latest quake-proof standards, with wider and more massive pilars. Construction work proceeded apace and in September 1996, after just one-and-a-half years, the newly elevated route reopened to the great relief of Kobe's commuters.

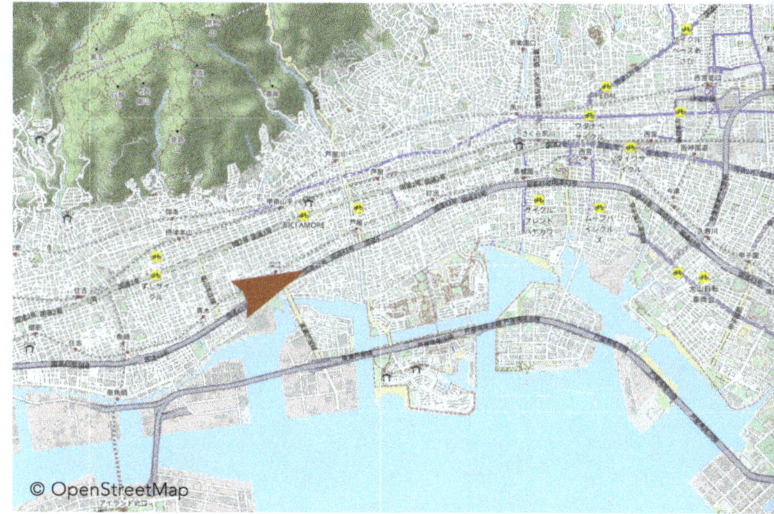

OSAKA

Kōrai-bashi

Osaka's Kōrai Bridge is one of a dozen bridges that during the Edo period used to straddle the Higashi Yokobori-*gawa*, the old Eastern Moat that used to form Osaka Castle's westernmost defense. The bridges were of strategic as well as economic importance, as they connected the Uemachi district on the west side of the castle's outer bailey to the commercial district of Senba. All except one of the bridges were burned during the siege of Osaka Castle in 1614-15. They were all rebuilt in the wake of the siege and remained in place up until the end of the Edo period.

Like Tokyo's Nihonbashi Bridge, Osaka's Kōrai Bridge formed the node in a network of highroads that included the Saigoku Kaidō toward the west, The Kyō Kaidō toward Kyoto, the Kuragari-*goe* Nara Kaidō toward Nara, and the Kishū Kaidō toward Wakayama. The bridge was erected by

Toyotomi Hideyoshi when he built his castle in the 1580s. He named it Kōrai Bridge after the Goryeo kingdom on the Korean Peninsula when a Korean embassy visited Osaka Castle during the late 16th century.

During the early Meiji period, the wooden bridge was replaced by a cast iron version. It was designed by Motoki Shōzō (1824–75). Shōzō was born into a family of Dutch interpreters in Nagasaki, but in the course of his Dutch studies, he developed a deep interest in Western engineering, in particular shipbuilding and steel manufacture. That interest led him to get involved in printing, which in turn led him to begin research on movable type at the local steelworks of the Nagasa Seitetsu-*sho*. To learn more, he invited the Shanghai-based Presbyterian minister William Dill Gamble (1830–68) to Nagasaki. Using Gamble's method of producing metal printing plates by way of electrotyping, the two men eventually managed to develop Japanese movable

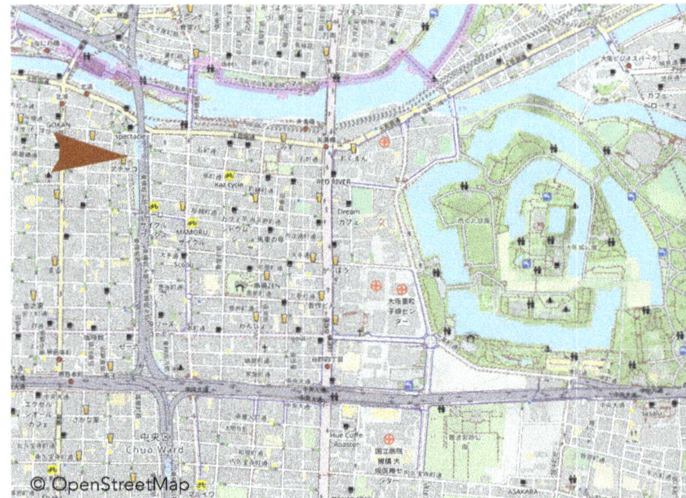

type. It was such a success that, in 1870, Motoki was able to open a branch office in Osaka. The Osaka Kappan-*sho*, or the Osaka Print Shop, was

OSAKA – Kōrai-bashi

located on the city's Ote-*dōri*, the avenue that runs from the Eastern Moat to the Ōte-*mon*, the castle's western main gate.

It was shortly after he arrived in Osaka that Motoki was approached to design a new, cast-iron bridge. This he did. There were, however, no foundries yet in Japan that could cast the large pillars and girders to support such a bridge. And thus he approached his old Nagasaki acquaintance William John Alt (1840–1909), a British merchant-adventurer who had established himself in Nagasaki as a commission agent trading in ships, weapons, and tea. Alt had by now become so successful that he had

established his own trading company under the name W.J. Alt & Co. Alt had the structures cast in England and shipped them over to Osaka. As can be imagined, the project was a costly affair, so costly, indeed, that it led to a small diplomatic row.

Installed in 1870, the cast-iron Kōrai Bridge stood until 1929, when it was replaced by the current steel-reinforced concrete bridge. Since then, the bridge has become overshadowed by the Hanshin Expressway No 1, whose pylons rudely plod the course of the Eastern Moat until, at the Higashisenba Junction, they unite with the Hanshin Expressway No 13.

Ebisu-bashi

Osaka is a city of moats and its best-known bridge is the Ebisu-*bashi*, the reason being that it is closely associated with Dōton-*bori*, Osaka's popular night-time entertainment area. The name Dōton-*bori* refers to Osaka's southern moat along which much of the entertainment is situated and across which the bridge sits. The moat was named after Yasui Dōton (1533–1615), one of four local entrepreneurs who hatched a plan to connect the Eastern Moat to the Kizu River and turn the Senba district into an island onto itself. The main aim was to improve access over water toward the area and thereby promote its commerce. Hygiene, too, was a consideration. The moat simply terminated in a dead end toward the south; and this while many of the city's open sewers disgorged their waste right into the moat, turning it into an infernal cesspit that produced such a stench in summer that it made life in the southern reaches of Uemachi and Senba unbearable.

Work on the project was begun in 1612, when all but the most western section of the moat was excavated. It ground to a halt during the siege and

was resumed shortly afterward, not by Dōton, who had been killed during the siege, but by his fellow entrepreneurs, who named the moat in his honor when it was completed toward the end of 1615.

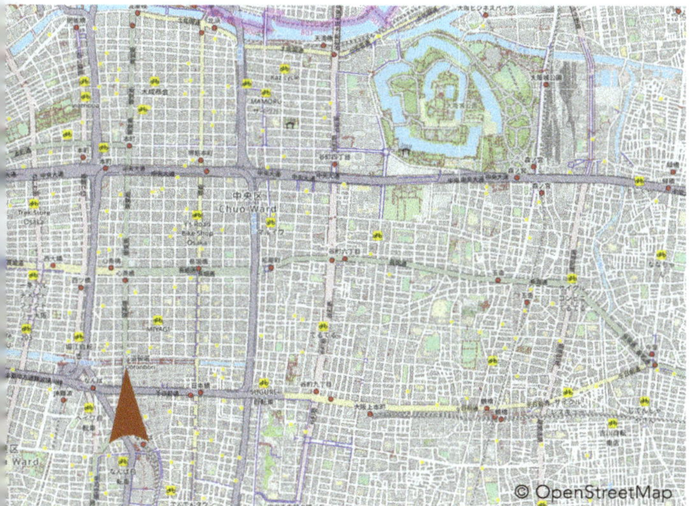

OSAKA – Ebisu-bashi

Dōton-bori

It was Dōton's fellow entrepreneurs, too, who laid the groundwork for the area's entertainment scene when, to promote trade through the moat, they moved the theaters from nearby Nanba to the south bank of Dōton-*bori*. In many cases, the term 'theater' was a bit of a misnomer. The main form of staged popular entertainment at the time was *kabuki*, comic playlets about everyday life. The roles were initially played by women, who played both female and male roles. The ribaldry and sexual innuendo of these plays attracted huge crowds, especially since many 'actresses' made a handsome living on the side by playing more intimate roles. As a result, their art was also known as *yūjo kabuki*, or 'prostitute *kabuki*.' It was banned by the authorities in 1629. After that, all roles had to be played by men. They, too, didn't shy away from a bit of

カベ
DRUG &
COSMETIC
TAX FREE
免税
Japan.
Tax-free
Shop
壁薬粧店
カべ
道頓堀中央薬店
1F
2F
禁止
当り
秘宝館
神戸牛
金龍ラーメン本店
日本一射的場
射的
道頓堀 新世界 秘宝館
戦後大阪府公認射的場一号店
実弾禁止やで!!
CHIBO
ステーキ
すき焼き
しゃぶしゃぶ
和ノ宮
WANOMIYA
射的
1~6F

Looking eastward along
Dōton-*bori* today

action on the side so that, in 1652, *wakashū kabuki*, or 'teenager *kabuki*,' was also outlawed. After that, just a few officially recognized theaters were allowed to operate at Dōton-*bori*: the Naniwa-*za*, the Naka-*za*, the Kaku-*za*, the Asahi-*za*, and the Benten-*za*. They were collectively known as the Goza, or the Five Theaters. The staged *kabuki* and *ningyō jōruri* (puppet) performances were advertised on large banners attached to *yagura*, or turrets that were erected over their entrances, reasons for which they were also known as the Go-*yagura*. Not one of the Goza has survived: some were sold off, some were turned into movie theaters, one burned down while it was being dismantled.

OSAKA – -Dōton-bori

Left: Looking eas along Dōton-*bori*, with the Kaku-*za* in the foreground and the Asahi-*za* in the distance

Below: Looking north across the Shinsai-*bashi*. In the distance one can see the massive roofs of the Minamimi-*dō* and the Kitami-*dō* temples

Shinsai-bashi

Crossing the Ebisu-*bashi* and passing through the roofed shopping street would bring one to the Shinsai-*bashi*. This bridge spanned the Nagahori-*gawa*, the old moat that separated the northern island of Senba from the southern island of Shima no Uchi. The bridge derived its name from Okada Shinsai (1575–1639). Shinsai's grandfather had been a samurai in the service of Oda Nobunaga and had played an important part in pacifying the Ise Peninsula. It had also cost him his life. Shinsai's father had abandoned samurai life and moved to Fushimi and become a merchant.

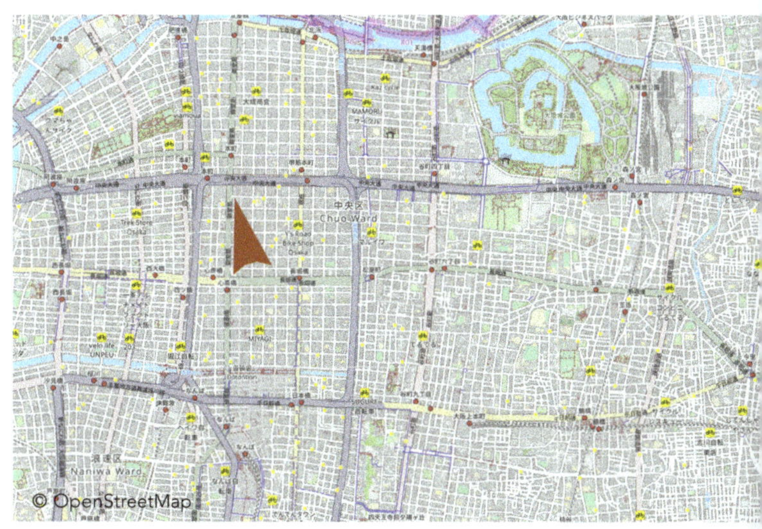

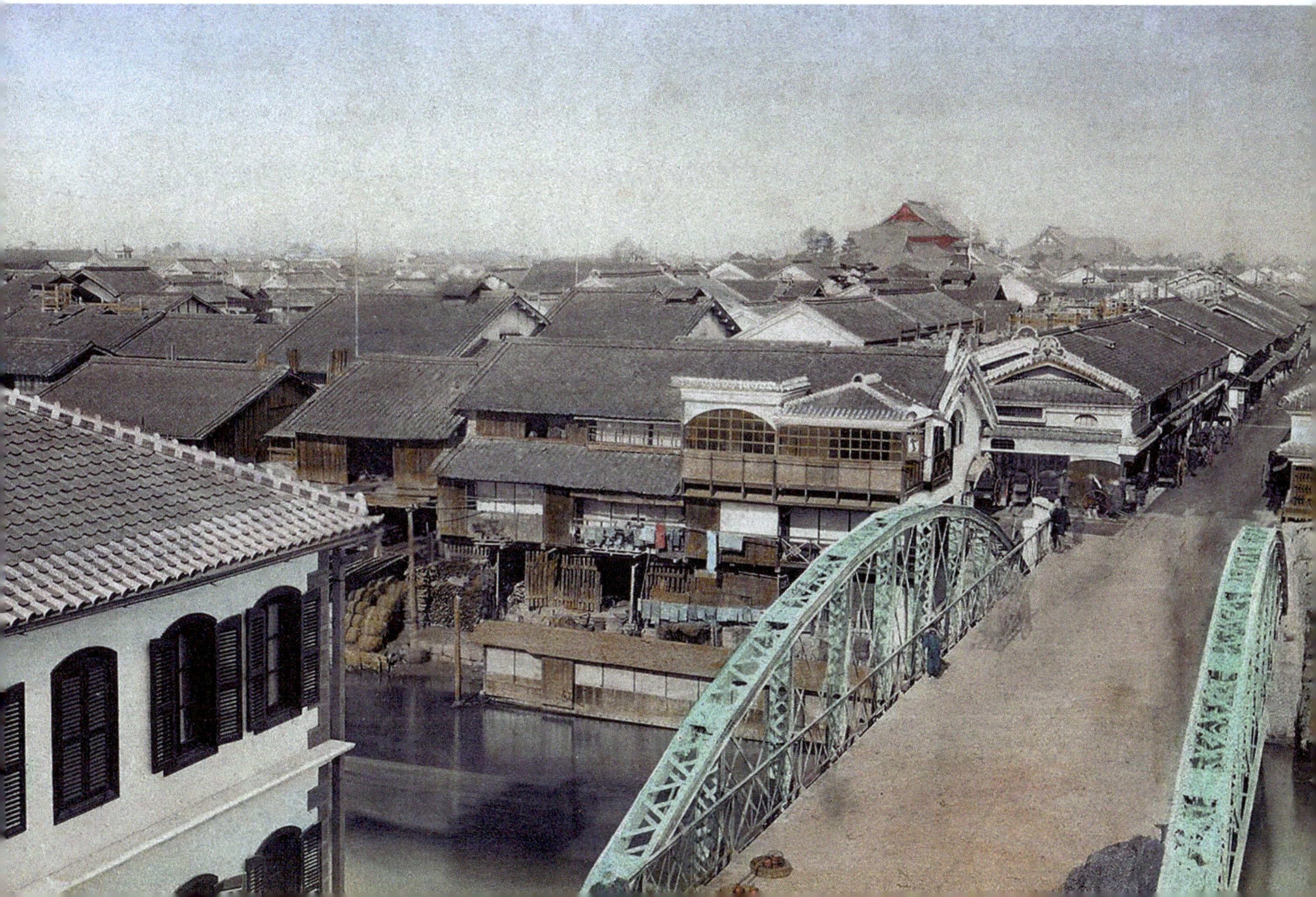

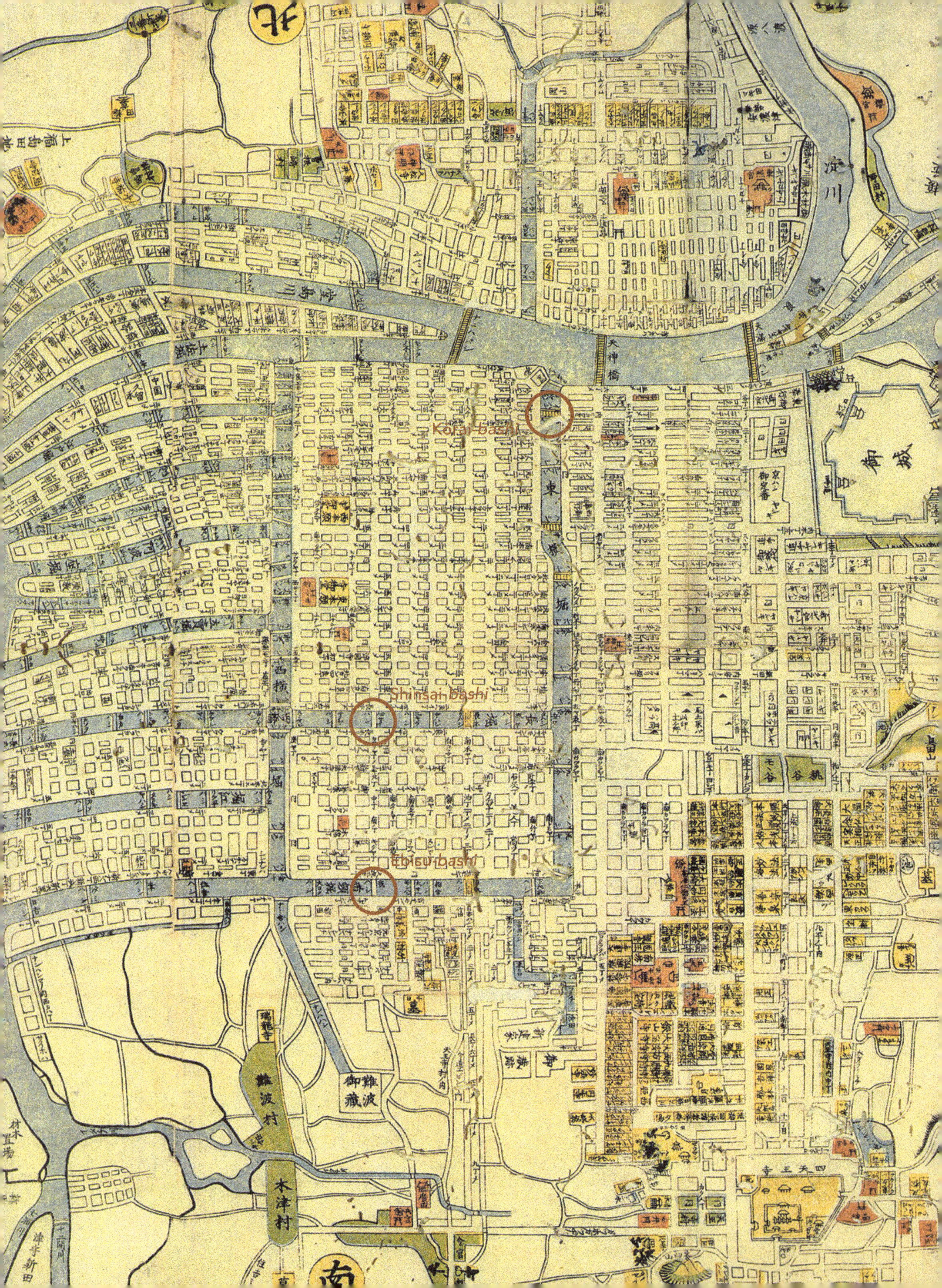

淀川
天神橋
Korai-bashi
Shinsai-bashi
Ebisu-bashi
難波村
木津村
御蔵
瑞龍寺

Shinsai smelled an opportunity when it presented itself. When Tokugawa Ieyasu laid siege to Osaka Castle in the winter of 1614, the young merchant formed a conglomerate of traders who supplied the warlord's army with arms and provisions. In reward, he was commissioned with the reconstruction (the town had been laid waste in the fighting) of the merchant townships on the two islands. He widened the Nagahori Moat to improve traffic and built a bridge across it to reconnect the two islands.

He wasn't the modest type, either, naming the new bridge after himself. He settled along the Nahahori-gawa, not far from his bridge, conducting a highly lucrative trade in products from all over the country. He passed away a very wealthy man at the age of sixty-four.

For two-and-a-half centuries Shinsai's creation stood, though its wooden beams would have been replaced many times. But in 1873, three years after the Kōrai Bridge had been cast in iron, Shinsai's bridge underwent the same treatment. This time, perhaps because of the diplomatic row over the

high costs for the former, its parts were ordered from Germany. Unlike the Kōrai Brdige, the new Shinsai bridge was a bowstring suspension bridge whose sections were riveted together.

The steel Shinsai Bridge stood until 1909, when it was replaced by a **steel-reinforced concrete bridge**. That bridge survived the devastation of the Second World War but when, in 1964, the Nagahori Moat was filled in, the bridge became obsolete and was dismantled. Today, the site of

the former bridge is one of Osaka's busiest pedestrian crossings. The Shinsaibashi-*tsūji*, the shopping mall that connects it to the Ebisu Bridge is the city's most popular shopping mall.

Thus the memory of the enterprising merchant lives on. The German-made steel bridge also survives. In 1973, to celebrate the bridge's 100th anniversary, its carefully preserved sections were moved nine kilometers northeast of its original location and reassembled as a **pedestrian flyover** at the Tsurumi Ryuakuchi Park. It is believed to be the oldest surviving steel bridge in Japan.

KYOTO

Kiyomizu-dera

Kyoto's best-loved temple is undoubtedly the Kiyomizu Temple. With a main hall that sits on a raised platform on stilts up to twelve meters long, it has captured the imagination of visitors ever since it was founded in 778 by a priest from Nara's Kōfuku Temple by the name of Enshin. The temple derived its name from a small waterfall, whose 'pure waters' still cascade down the Higashi-*yama* slopes to this day. Most of the temple's surviving structures are from a later date, the main hall having been built in 1633.

The expression *Kiyomizu no butai kara tobioriru*, or 'to jump off the Kiyomizu platform' is the equivalent of the English expression 'to take the plunge.'

The Japanese version originated in the belief that, if one survived the 14-meter plunge, one's wishes would be granted. Many have actually done so, at least 235 people, according to records kept by the temple during the Edo period. Some 200 survived the jump, though the records do not tell us whether their wishes came true. The custom had already been banned for two decades when the Tokyo-based photographer Ezaki Reiji set up his camera on the opposite balcony of the Okunoin.

Ezaki Reiji (1845–1910) lost both his parents at a young age. He was raised by his uncle, who farmed a small plot of land on the east bank of the Nagara River in what is today Gifu Prefecture. At the age of eighteen, he moved to Ōgaki, where he studied photography under a chemist and photographer by the name of Kuze Jisaku. In 1870, he moved to Tokyo, where he rented a room and opened a small photographic studio, but soon ran into financial difficulties. With a loan of ¥600, he managed to relocate his studio

to the popular location of Asakusa, from which moment onward his business began to prosper. During the early eighties, when he began using imported gelatin dry plate negatives, making him a so-called 'quick photographer,' his business evolved into Asakusa's best-known portrait studio. Later in his career, he began to travel, to Kamakura, Kyoto, Osaka, and all the way down to Nagasaki.

Yasaka-jinja

A pleasant half-hour stroll northward through Kyoto's temple-studded suburbs along the Higashi-*yama* slopes, stands the Yasaka Shrine. Its Nishi-Sakura-*mon*, the huge red gate at its western entrance, looks out over Shijō-*dōri*, the old capital's fourth main (east-west) avenue. Shijō-*dōri* forms the northern border of Kyoto's Gion-*machi*. The district came into being during the Warring States period, when pilgrims visiting the Yasaka Shrine needed a roof over their heads, food in their stomachs, and some diversion after they had offered prayers at the shrine. During the Edo period, diversion came to take precedence over worship and Gion became the capital's main geisha district.

The Yasaka Shrine itself has a long history. It is said to have its origins in the Hean period, when, in 876, a monk from Nara by the name of Ennyo founded a temple on the east bank of the Kamo River. Shortly before that, in 869, the realm had been visited by a plague. To appease the gods of pestilence, the suffering citizens invoked the help of Gozu Tennō, the Gion cult's god of healing, who came down from Higashi-*yama* (the mountains east of the capital) and chose the temple grounds as

his new abode. The area where he chose to reside
was known as Yasaka, or Eight Slopes. Ever since,
the Gion Matsuri, a festival celebrating the capital's
deliverance from the plague, has evolved around
the Yasaka Shrine built in his honor.

When Adolfo Varsari set up his camera on the
steps of the shrine in 1886 to photograph Shijō-
dōri, the two *komainu*, the fearsome lion-dogs on
their rectangular pedestals guarding the entrance,
stil stood in front of the huge Nishi-Sakura Gate.
Crafted out of stone, they had been erected four
years earlier. In 1926, they were replaced by bronze
komainu after the gate had received two flanking

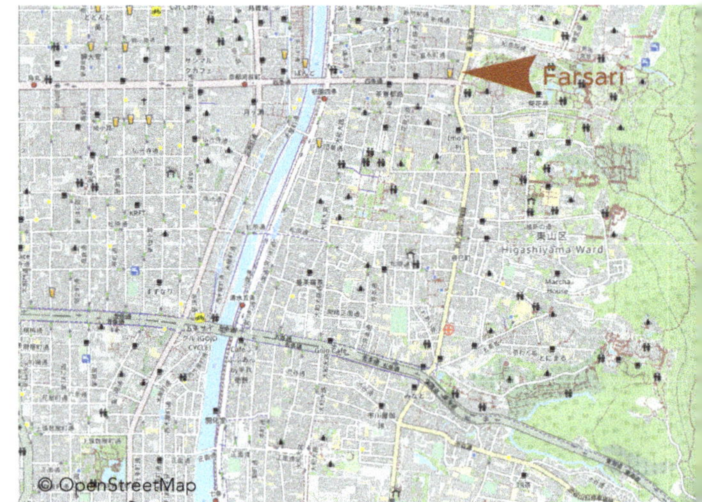

KYOTO – Yasaka-jinja

Left: Vasari's 1886 photograph taken from the steps of the Yasaka Shrine, looking westward along Shijō-*dōri*

Below: Looking toward the Yasaki Shrine from Shijō-*dōri* during the early Meiji period. The old *komainu* are still guarding the front of the Nishi-Sakura Gate

transepts the year before. The stone *komainu* were moved up the flight of stairs and now sit just inside the gate. Since then, the western entrance to the temple has been protected by four *komainu*.

Adolfo Farsari (1841–98) was born in Vicenza, Lombardy–Venetia (then still part of the Austrian Empire. He started out as a cavalryman in the Italian army but emigrated to the United States in 1863. A fervent abolitionist, he joined the Union Army and fought in the Civil War, but when his marriage failed, he left his wife and two children and moved to Yokohama, Japan. There, he teamed up with E.A. Sargent, a

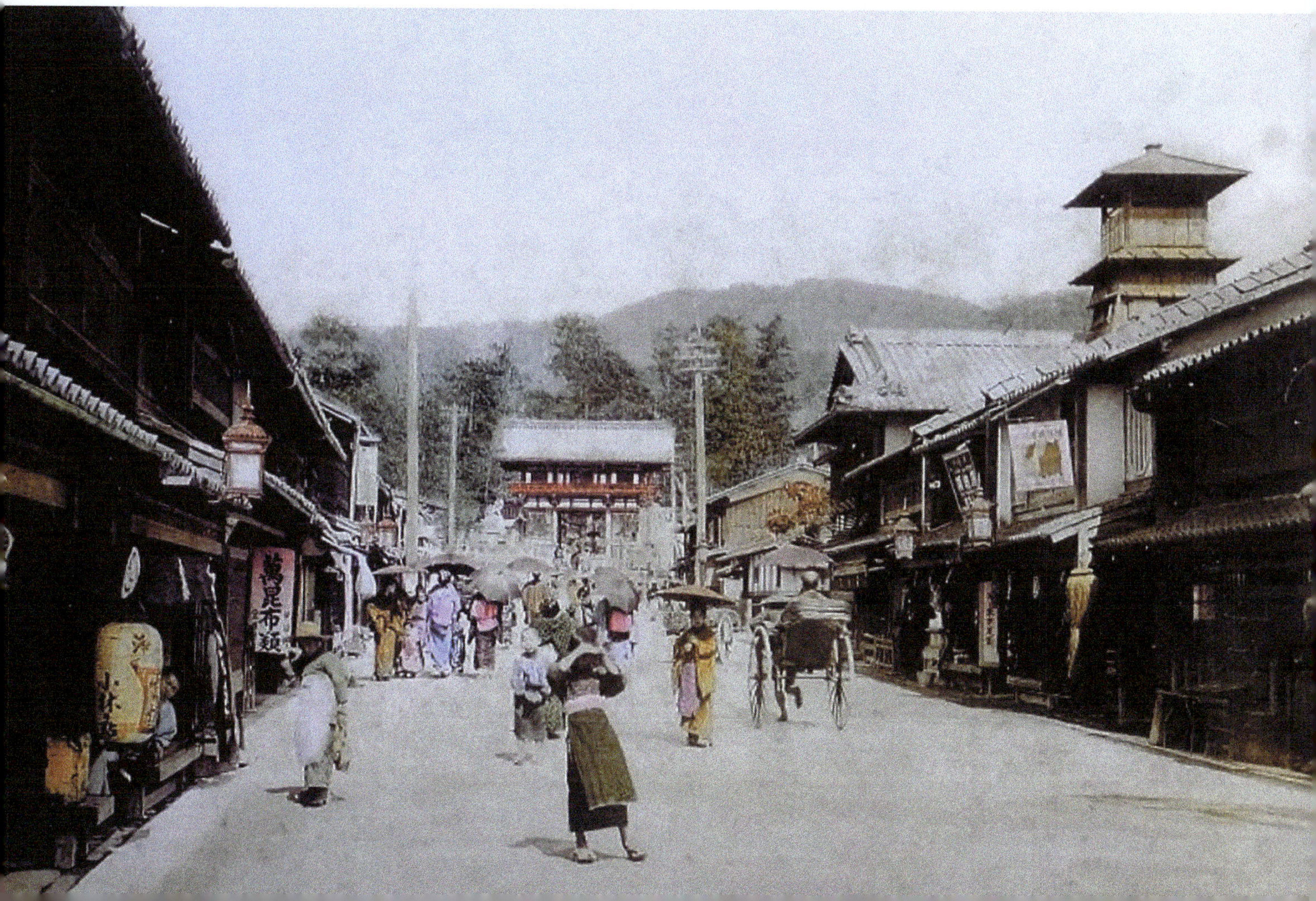

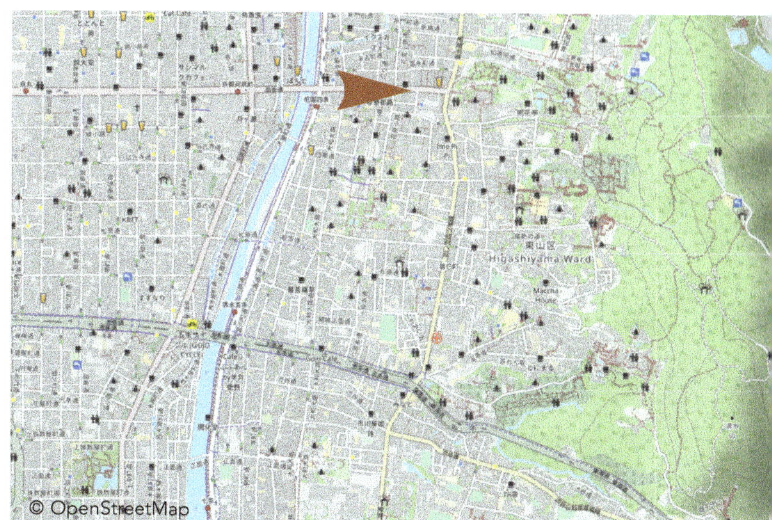

Below: The Yasaka Shrine today, with the original *komainu* sitting inside the Nishi-Sakura Gate

Right: Looking northward along the Kamo River from Shijō Ōhashi during the early Meiji period

newsagent and tobacconist, who also published photographic albums. By the time the partnership broke down, in 1883, Farsari had taught himself the art of photography. Together with the Japanese photographer Tamamura Kōzaburō (1856–1923), he acquired the studio of Raimund von Stillfried and Hermann Andersen, thus inheriting part of the legacy of Felice Beato. This partnership, too, broke up, and Farsari continued on his own. When, in 1886, a fire destroyed his studio, he traveled around Japan to replenish his photographic library, which by the end of the decade com-

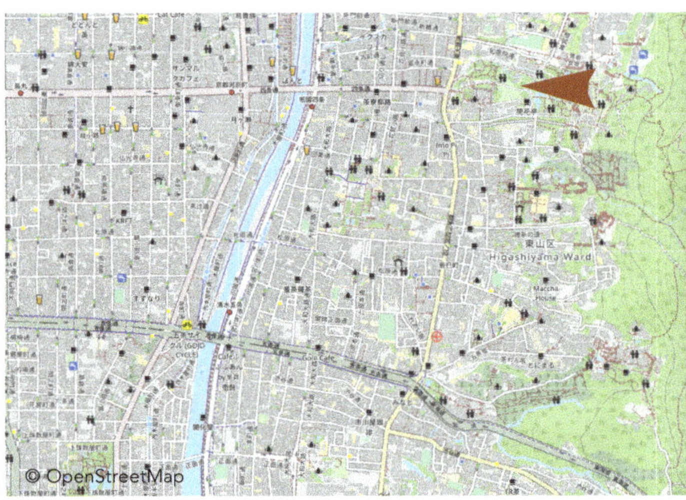

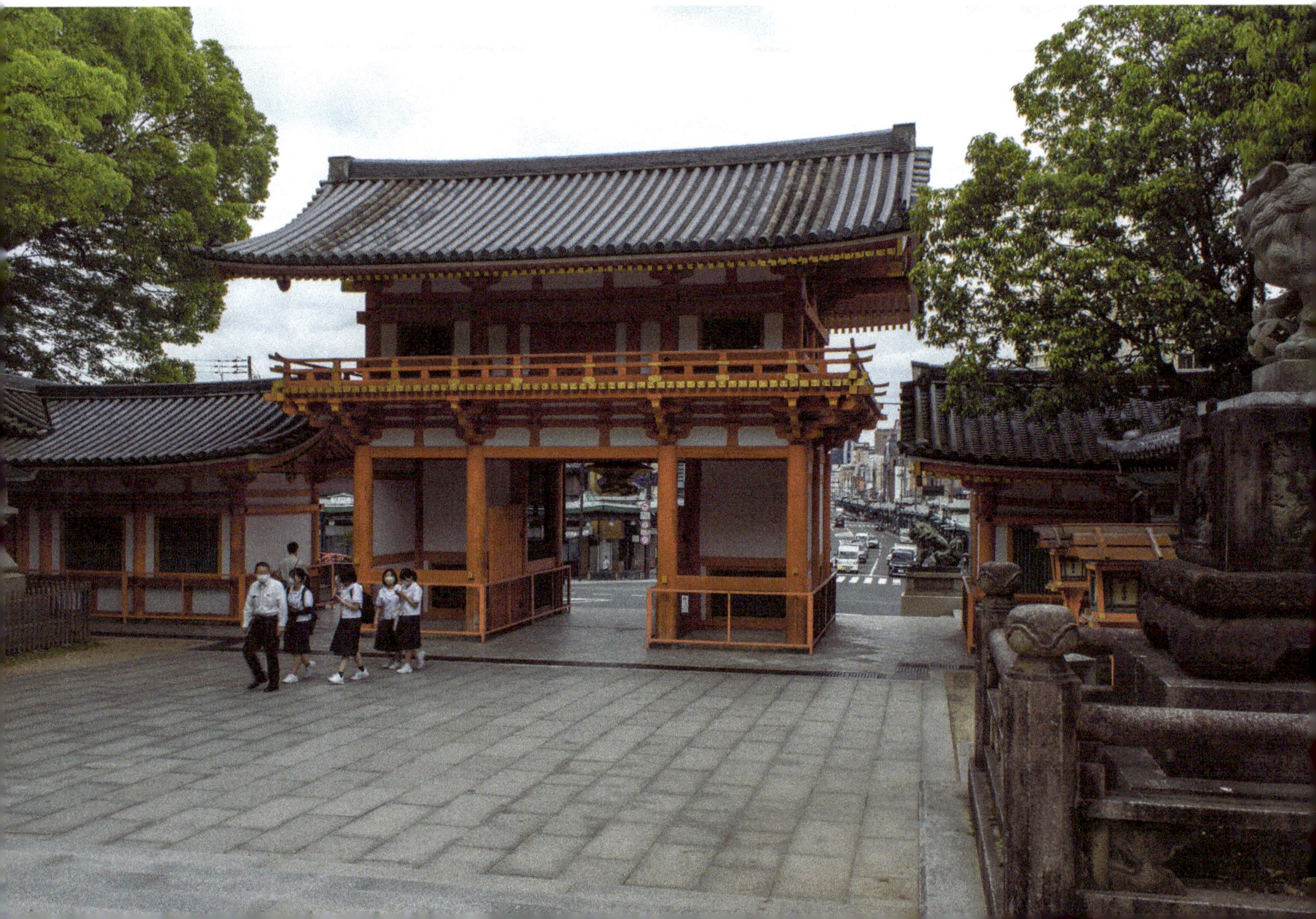

prised some 1000 images. When, in 1890, he left Japan for Italy, Farsari & Co. was the only foreign-owned studio, with agents in Kobe and  Nagasaki. It continued to operate under his name until, a year later, it was acquired by his associate Tonokura Tsunetarō.

Kamo-gawa

A few minute's walk eastward along Shijō-*dōri* from the Yasaka Shrine, the old avenue crosses the Kamo River by way of the Shijō Ōhashi. North of the bridge, all along the west bank of the river toward the Sanjō Ōhashi, the river was lined by restaurants.

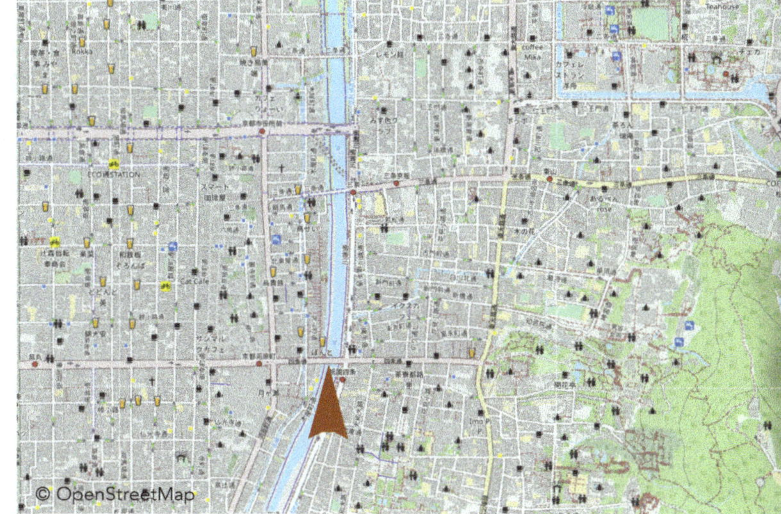

KYOTO – Kamo-gawa

Looking northward along the Kamo
River from Shijō Ōhashi today

During the early Edo period, their owners were allowed to erect so-called *nōryōyuka*, wooden platforms cantilevering over the river on stilts. Here customers were able to enjoy the river while eating and feasting during the Gion Matsuri. The custom became such a hit that more and more restaurants erected platforms so that, by the middle of the Edo period, the river was lined by *nōryōyuka* from Nijō to Gojō Ōhashi. Initially, they lined both sides of the river, but when, during the Taishō period, the Keihan railway line was extended from Sanjō to Demachi, the platforms on the left bank of the river had to be dismantled.

Too shallow for marine traffic, the river's main function has always been one of diversion. Every now and then, it burst its banks, washing the platforms away in a deluge. But the platforms returned, and with each new spring new revelers were drawn to the river's soothing waters. Enjoying one's lunch while listening to the river pass underneath became so popular that the *nōryōyuka* were even installed in the shade of the river's bridges. It was only during the 1970s that the river's increasingly poor water quality drove the revelers away. The wooden platforms disappeared. Thus a centuries-old tradition passed away, as did the even older custom of washing the silks fabrics of kimono in the river and drying them on its sand banks.

Lately, the water quality has improved again, and the *nōryōyuka* have returned. So have the revelers. Students of Kyoto University, whose campuses are situated on the river's east bank, have even coined a special word for their favorite pastime. They call it Kamo-*chiru*: to 'chill out along the Kamo River.'

NARA

Sanjō-dōri

Just like Kyoto, Nara, its predecessor as capital of the realm, was designed in the image of the ancient Chinese capitals, with the imperial palace firmly at its northern head and the city's avenues laid out in grid-like fashion before it. Much in the old city has changed over the centuries, but the grid-like pattern is still there, as is the Sanjō-*dōri*, the Third Avenue, which runs east-west from the grounds of

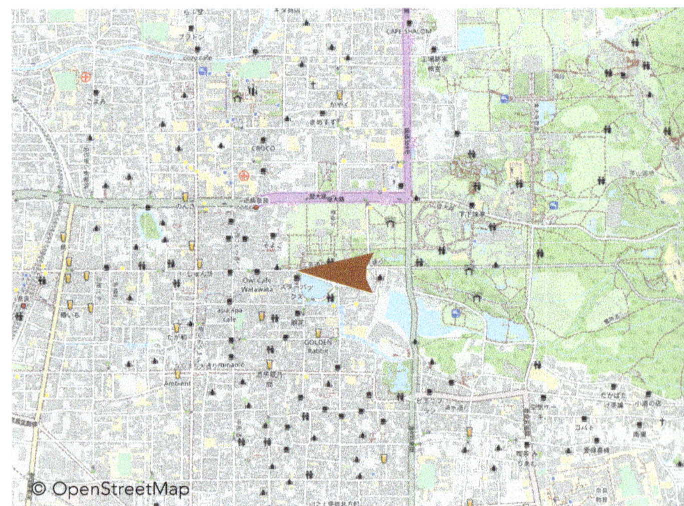

the Kasuga Taisha, along the grounds of the Kōfuku Temple and the Surusawa Pond, all the way to the Saho-*kawa*, the river that used to demarcate the old capital's western outskirts. There it went over in the Kuragarigoe Nara Kaidō, the old highroad that crossed the Ikoma Mountain range toward the Inland Sea. On the east side, it joined the Nara Kaidō and the Ise Kaidō, connecting the ancient to the new capital of Heian-kyō (Kyoto) and the pilgrim destination of the Ise Grand Shrine.

Nara's Sanjō-*dōri*, then, was an important thoroughfare. It still is. Today, it is Nara's main shopping avenue, lined with major retail outlets selling the world's top fashion brands alongside traditional stores selling kimonos, scrolls, tea, and Japanese confectionary. Only few of the 15 million tourists that visit the temple town each year can avoid

spending some money on Sanjō-*dōri*, if only to buy some cookies for the hundreds of tame deer that populate the city's greener areas.

NARA – Sanjō-dōri

NAGOYA

Atsuta-jingū

Nagoya's Atsuta-*jingū* has a history that is almost as old as that other famous shrine on the other side of the Ise Bay. That is, if we ignore the myth propagated by Japan's second-oldest history book, the *Nihon shoki*, which claims the Ise Grand Shrine was established some two thousand years ago by Yamatohime, the daughter of the legendary Emperor Suinin. In all probability, the first structure of the Ise Grand Shrine was erected somewhere between the late 5th and late 7th centuries. The Atsuta-*jingū*'s first structures, by contrast, are believed to have been erected in 646, but then again, that date is also based on less than bullet-proof historical records.

the shrine always enjoyed the patronage of powerful warrior clans. During the late 16th century, its high priests served the local Oda clan. On 12 June 1560, their leader, Oda Nobunaga, visited the shrine to offer prayers to the deities of war. He was about to do battle with the forces of Imagawa Yoshimoto, who was just then crossing through his territories to seize the capital of Kyoto. The warlord's prayers did not fall on deaf ears. That same day, he defeated a force ten times his own. Yoshimoto was killed, and Nobunaga was on his way to become Japan's new ruler.

Not only the shrine's history was closely linked to its locality; so was its architecture. Called Owari-*zukuri*, after the province of Owari (Aichi Prefecture), it is characterized by a layout in which the **main shrine** (*honden*) sits at the back, the liturgy hall (*saimonden*) in the middle, with a hall for worship

Whatever its true founding date, the Atsuta-*jingū* has a rich and fascinating history. Housing the Kusanagi no Tsurugi, the sacred sword of Yamato Takeru, a legendary prince of the Yamato dynasty,

(*haiden*) at the front. Another hallmark of the Owari-*zukuri* style of architecture was the V-shaped gable (*kiri-zuma*) roof with entrances (*tsuma-iri*) situated at the gable ends.

Below: The new, Shinmei-*zukuri* structures of the Atsuta Jingū

Right: The view from the ferry landing at Miya during the Edo period

But in 1893, the Meiji government, in one of its typical iconoclastic moves, decided to make the Atsuta-*jingū* resemble its pendant across the Ise Bay, the Grand Shrine at Ise, and to rebuild its structures in the native *shinmei-zukuri* style. It was something they had done before at the Itsukushima Shrine. There, it had been reversed during the Taishō era. But in Nagoya it stuck. Today, the only structure that retains some of the beautiful Owari-*zukuri* features is the Hikamianego-*jinja*, a shrine that is technically part of the Atsuta-*jingū* but stands some 10 km south of the complex at Higamiyama, on the south side of the Tenpaku River.

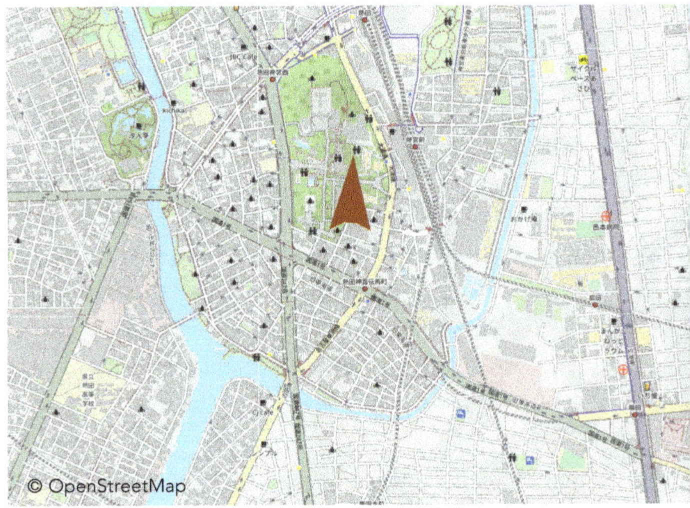

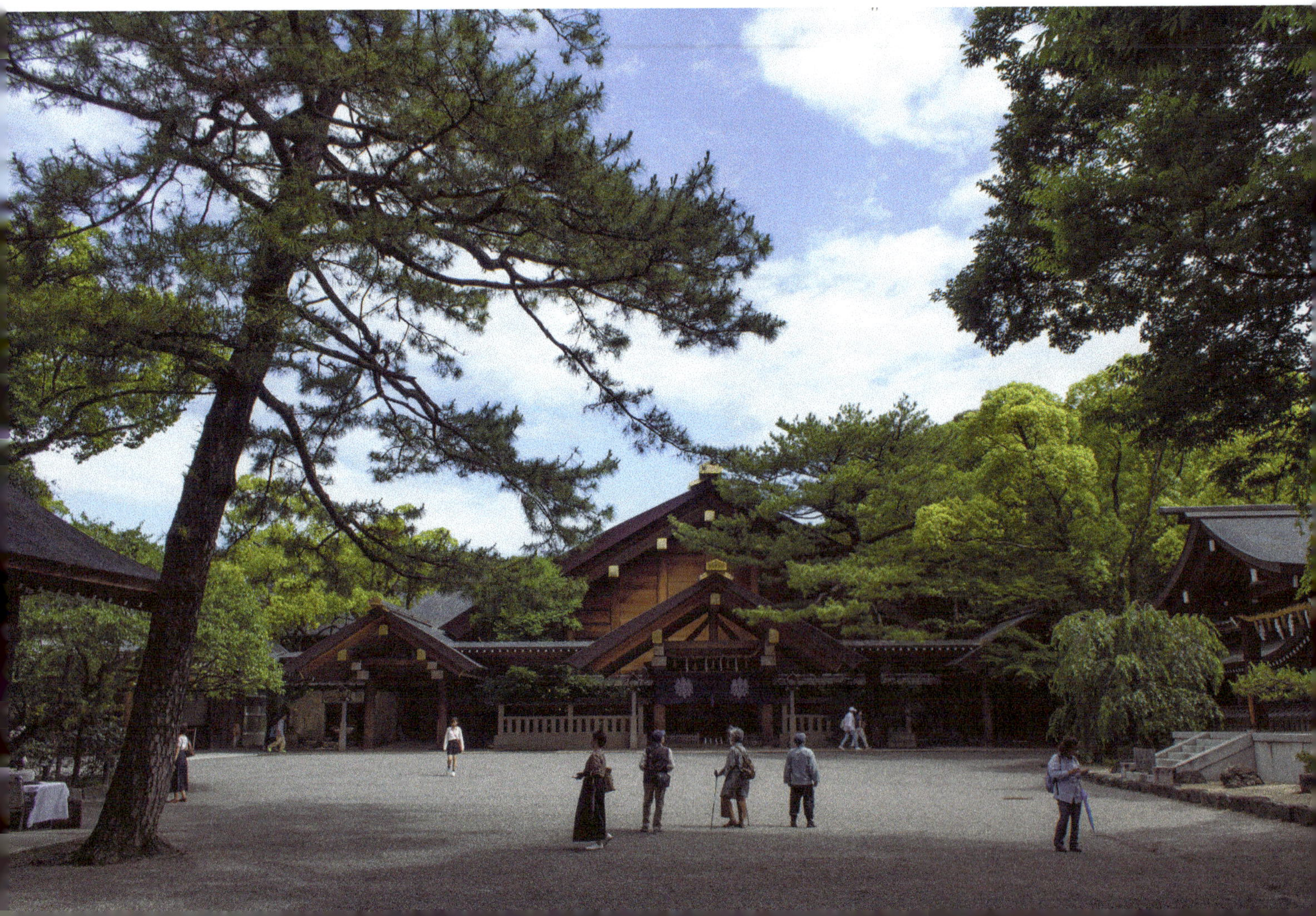

Miya-juku

The nearby post station of Miya was the place from where, during Japan's feudal era, many pilgrims disembarked to visit the Atsuta Shrine. For Miya was not only a post station but also a port. It sat at the east end of the so-called Shichiri no Watashi, the only leg in the five-hundred-kilometers-long Tōkaidō where its travelers had to cross over water. It was to avoid the wide estuary of the unpredictable Ibi and Kiso rivers that travelers coming down from Kyoto would embark from Kuwana on the west side of Ise Bay to have themselves ferried over to Miya. *Shichiri* means 'seven *ri*,' the distance over water between the two ports.

In those days, Miya lay directly along the bay. Today, its former ferry landing is still marked by the port's old lighthouse. It no longer casts its beam over the Bay of Ise, but has to make do with a wide canal that is carved through a 4 km-wide stretch of reclaimed land. But even then, it has not yet reached open water. Instead, it has to pass through

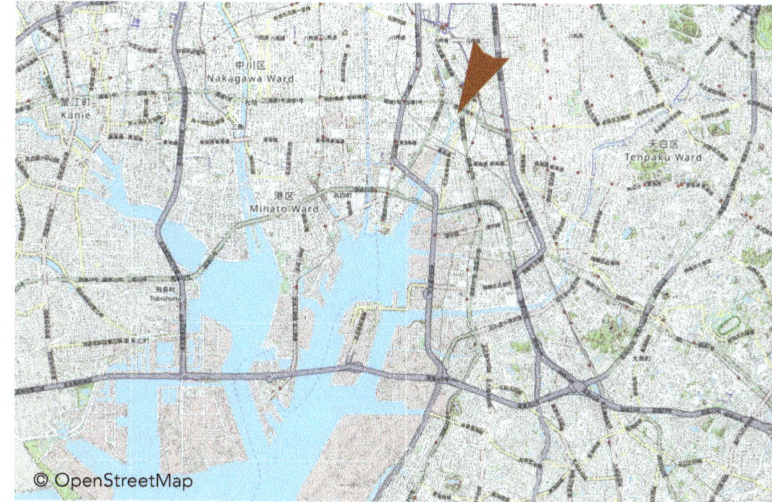

the Port of Nagoya, a vast harbor wedged in by yet more reclaimed land that is home to factories and port terminals.

Left: Only Miya's original lighthouse still marks the one-time ferry landing

Below: The Hori-kawa during the early Meiji period

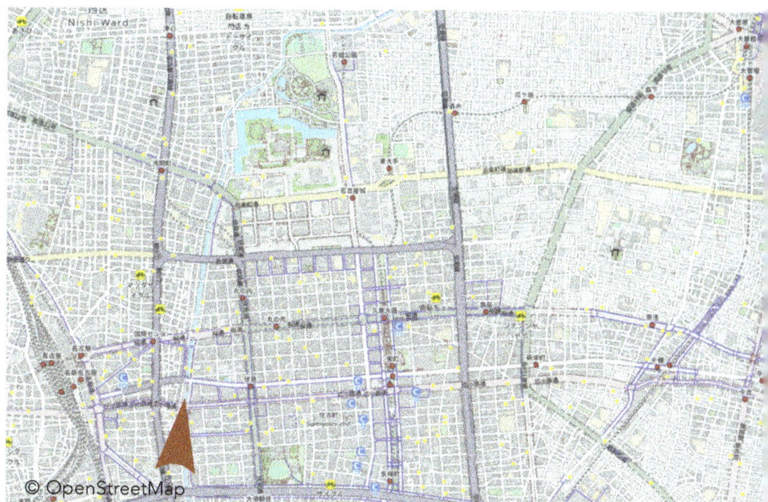

Hori-kawa

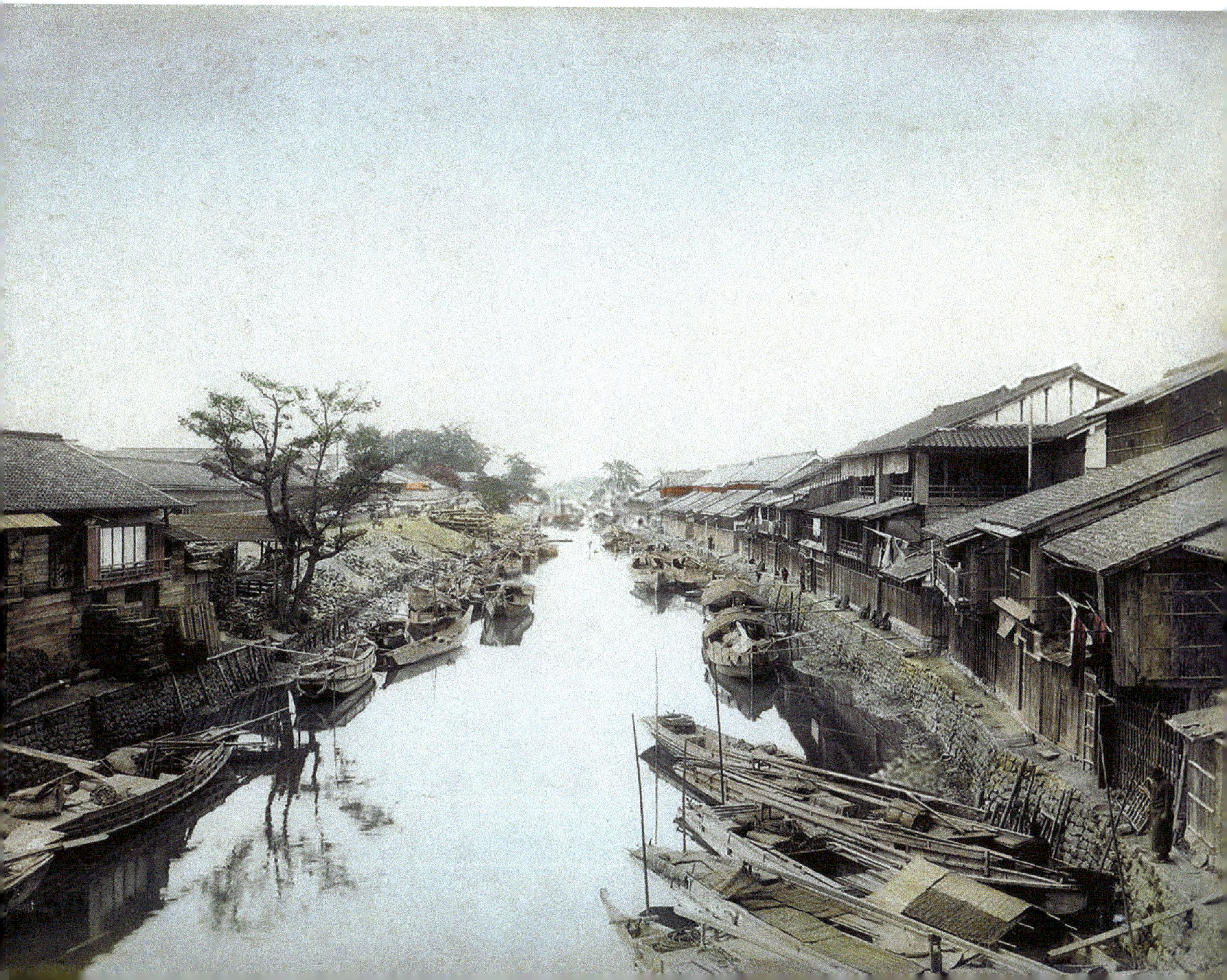

Miya was not necessarily the last port of call for vessels destined for Nagoya. Cargo destined for the city center could be carried up the Hori Canal, which extended from Miya, all the way to the outer moat of Nagoya Castle. It was the castle's expansion, in 1610, shortly after Shōgun Tokugawa Ieyasu's ninth son Tokugawa Yoshinao had been put in charge of the Owari domain, that led to the canal's creation. The canal was needed to transport the huge stones and beams that were harvested from around Ise Bay and beyond. It was one of the Edo period's major civil engineering projects. A huge force of laborers, under the supervision of Fukushima Masanori, spent three years digging the canal, though it is thought that the canal followed the route of a smaller existing stream that poured into Ise Bay west of Miya.

Half a century later, to improve the flow of water through the canal, the Hori-*kawa* was extended three kilometers northeast of the castle to make it connect with the Yada River, just before it joined the Shōnai River. More recently, various initiatives have led to a significant improvement in the canal's water quality. Every year, from late March to early June, tourists can book a passage on the Hori River Cruise. The 'cruise' will take them a mile upstream from Naya Bridge to the Asahi Bridge, which used to sit in the southwest corner of Nagoya Castle's inner citadel. Today, the castle grounds no longer reach that far, but it is only a five-minute walk from the bridge to the ticket booth of the castle's former inner citadel.

Sakae

It was Tokugawa Yoshinao's arrival in Nagoya that also lay at the birth of Nagoya's present-day downtown area of which the Sakae neighborhood is the most popular. Up until 1612, the castle town of Kiyosu, slightly northwest of Nagoya Castle, on the other side of the Shōnai River, had been the seat of Owari's *daimyō*. But when Ieyasu decided his son should reside in Nagoya, the Edo *bakufu* organized a wholesale move of Kiyosu's commercial district. Close to three thousand households of

retainers, merchants, and artisans were moved, lock, stock, and barrel, to Nagoya's newly created Sotobori, Horikiri, Misono, and Hisaya townships (roughly the area covered by today's Marunouchi Ward). Not only that, more than a hundred temples and shrines were dismantled, moved to Nagoya, and reassembled to complement its dozen or so existing structures.

Sakae's main avenues of Hirokōji and Hisaya Ōdōri, which intersect just south of Nagoya's landmark TV Tower, both go back to this period. **Hirokōji** still bears the name by which it was known

in those days. It ran due east from the above-mentioned Naya Bridge across the Hori Canal. Hisaya Ōdōri roughly coincides with Hisaya-*machi*, the thoroughfare that ran due south from the castle's southeast corner. Hisaya, in Japanese, literally means 'eternal shops' or 'shops forever,' a name that was bestowed on the avenue by Tokugawa Yoshinao in the hope it would become a self-fulfilling prophecy. This it certainly proved to be, for many of the merchants who had been uprooted

NAGOYA – Sakae

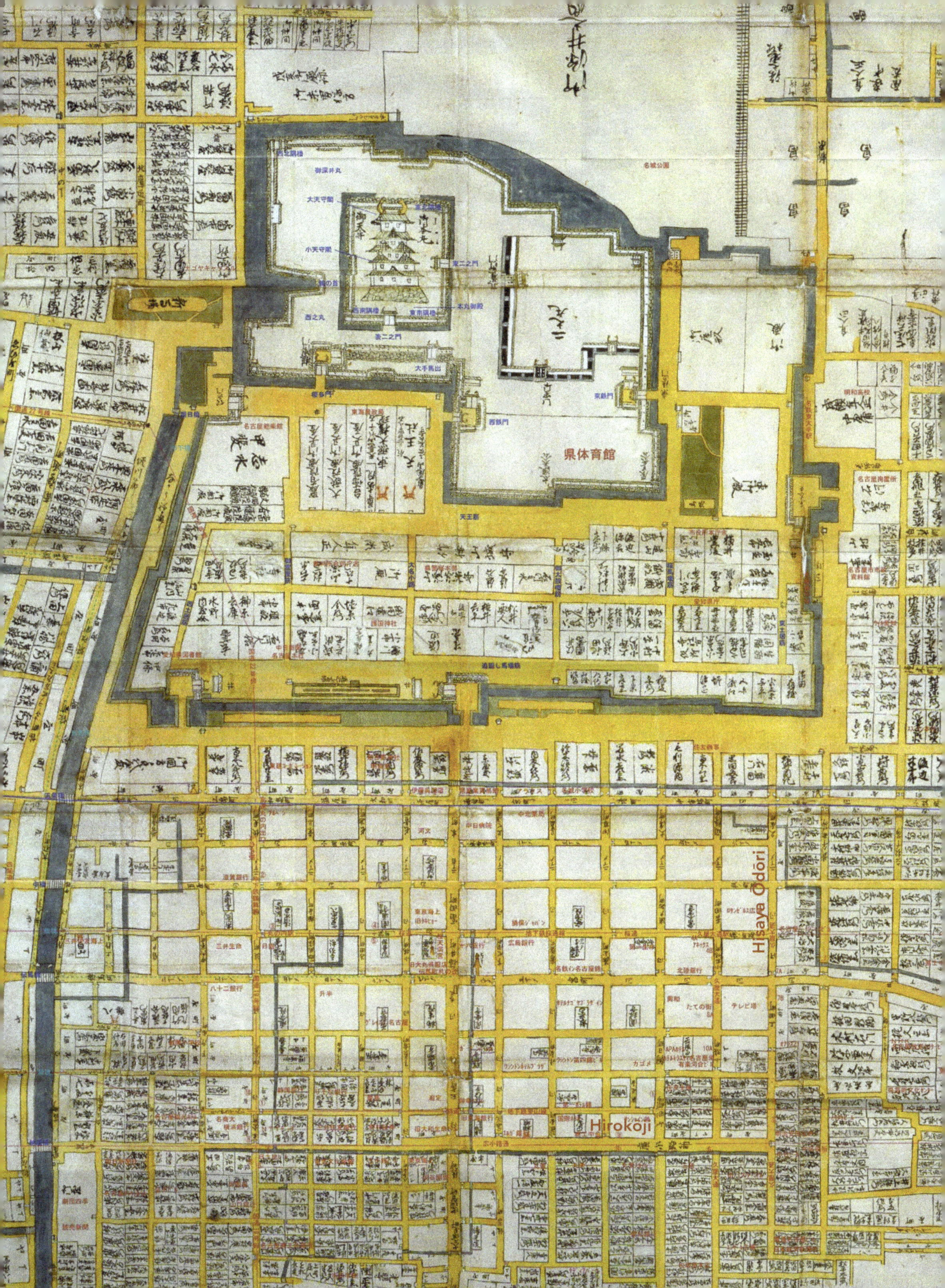
名城公園
県体育館
Hisaya Ōdōri
Hirokoji

Below: Looking down Hirokōji from the Sakae Intersection during the Taishō period

Right: The Sakae Intersection today

from Kiyosu settled in this area. Sakae as we know it today—Nagoya's central business district—really came into its own during the Meiji period, when local government offices, schools, restaurants and, last but not least, big Japanese retail stores established themselves in the area.

The real heart of the area is the Sakae Intersection, which sits at the crossroads of Hirokōji and Ōstu-*dōri*, just one block west from Hisaya Ōdōri. It has undergone many changes throughout the last one-and-a-half century, the most dramatic being those during the Meiji period and in the wake of the Second World War.

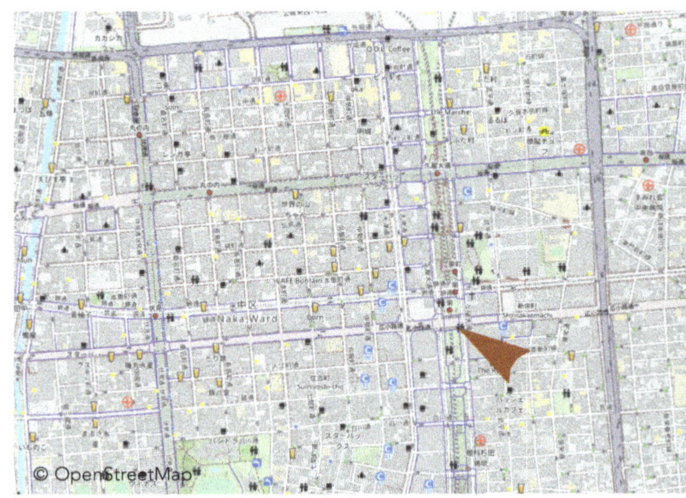

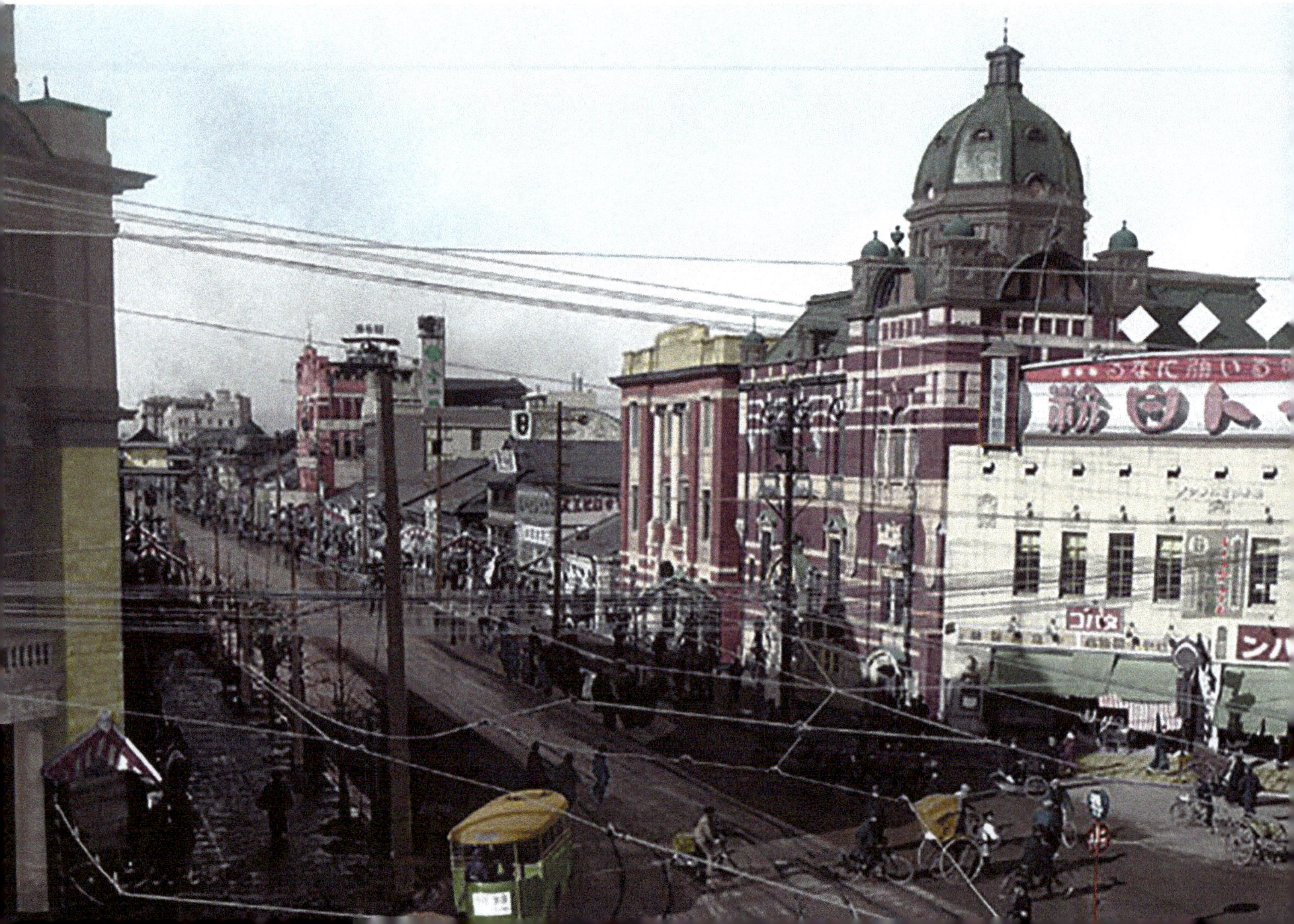

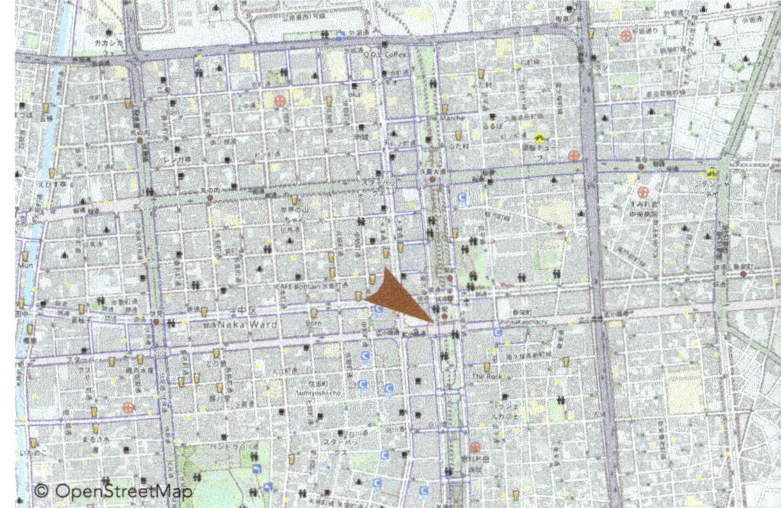

Today's layout of Nagoya's downtown area is the result of Allied air raids during the last months of the war, which laid most of the city (and its castle) in ashes and killed close to twelve thousand of its citizens. Much of the destruction was caused by firestorms in the wake of the incendiary bombing. This led to a plan by its city planners to create two, one-hundred-yard-wide, structure-free barriers to prevent fire from spreading from one city area to the other. One of these was the Wakimiya Ōdori, which runs east-west along Nagoya's Shirakawa Park. The other was the old Hisaya Ōdōri. As a result, the city was effectively cut into four quarters into which the fire could be contained.

NAGOYA – *Sakae*

SHIZUOKA

Satta-tōge

for a long time, the Satta Pass, just a few kilometers north of Shizuoka City, was one of the Tōkaidō's main hurldes. *Satta*, or '*sattva*' in Sanskrit, means 'pure' or 'divine.' It is also shorthand for bodhisattva or 'enlightened being.' According to legend, the pass took its name from a stone statue of the bod-hisattva (*jizō*) that found its way into the net of a local fisherman and has been venerated by fish-ermen ever since.

During Japan's long period of civil strife, the pass became the scene of hard fighting when the feudal warlord Takeda Shingen from the landlocked province of Kai sought to open up a route to the

sea. He crossed the pass twice. First in 1568, when he pursued the Imagawa westward to Sunpu (Shizuoka). They had to retreat and the town was sacked. But when, the next year, he sought to retrace his steps across the pass to intercept the

Hōjō (who had come to the aid of the Imagawa) he was stopped in his tracks and forced to withdraw his troops again to Kai.

The pass remained a bottleneck right up until the end of the 19th century. But in 1886 the Meiji government decided to build the Tōkaidō Honsen, or the Tōkaidō Main Line, a railway line that would connect the former capital of Kyoto to the new capital of Tokyo by following the route of the Tōkaidō highway. Parts of the new railway line (between Kyoto and Ōtsu, and between Tokyo and Yokohama) had already been built, and it took only three years for the two cities to be linked. The stretch between Kōzu (near Odawara) and Shizuoka circumvented the Hakone Mountains by making a detour along Gotenba (north of Mt. Fuji), but navi-gated the Satta Pass through a short tunnel through

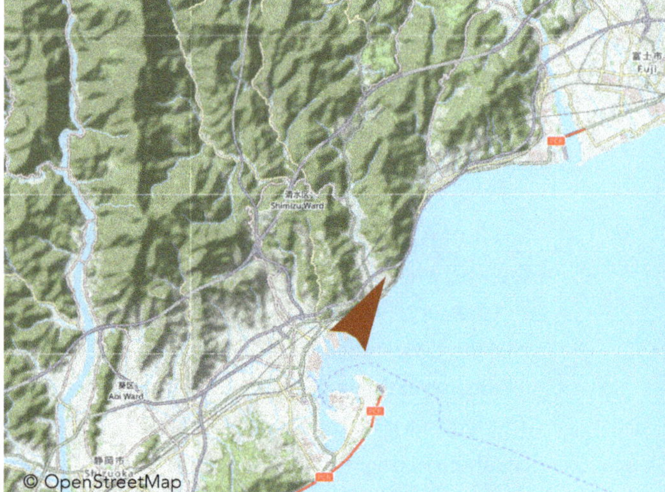

the sea-side slope. Only a narrow footpath allowed those on foot or bicycle to traverse the pass on level ground.

It took until 1934 before heavy traffic could use a paved road that abutted the sea by a low wall.

Just north of the pass, it cut across the railway tracks to pick up the old trail of the Tōkaidō. Since the Second World War, the pass has been subdued by the two-lane National Route 1, which cuts across the bay by way of the Fuji-Yūi Bypass; and the two-lane Tōmei Expressway, which cuts through the western part of the mountains by way of a 500-m tunnel. Those who whizz past on the *shinkansen* don't even get to see the pass but cut through the mountains by way of a three-section, 9-kilometers-long tunnel a kilometer inland from the pass.

FUJI

Imaizumi

It was while traveling down the Tōkaido during the 1880s that Kusakabe Kimbei took this image of Mt. Fuji. He had done the same at Ōmiya, another small hamlet along the Tōkaidō, due south from the mountain, just where the high road starts to ascend toward the Hakone Pas, as well as from nearby Numazu. Clearly, the majestic mountain,

which has watched over all those who make their way along the high road, captured the photographer's imagination, as it has done with millions of travelers before and after.

This image was taken from a hamlet called Imaizumi, on the west side of Suruga Bay, which has long since been swallowed up by the city named after the famed volcano: Fuji City. Many places in those days carried or included the name Izumi, which means 'spring' or 'fountain' in Japanese. Yet it is only from Imaizumi that the smaller volcano of Mt. Hōei, which sits on Fuji-san's southeast flank, stands out in such relief, making the mountain appear less symmetrical than from any other point along the Tōkaidō.

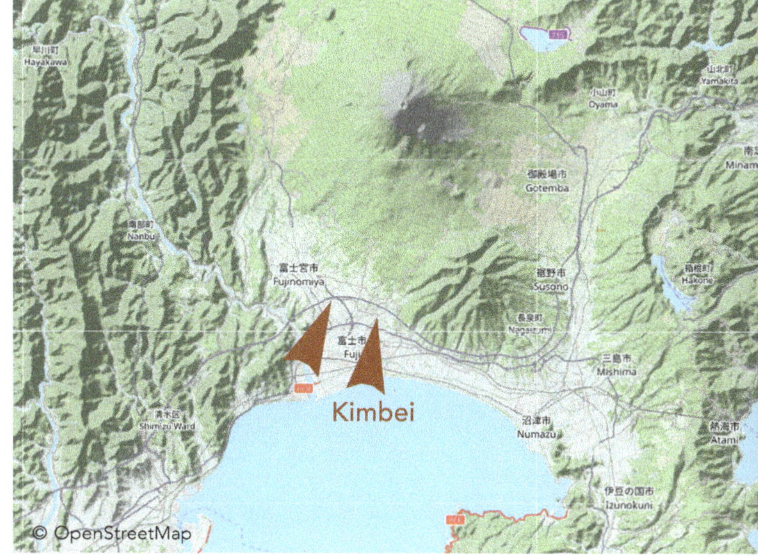

FUJI – Imaizumi

Tagonoura

Imaizumi was just a stroll away from the port of Tagonoura, the place where the Numa River pours into the Bay of Suruga. It was a regular port of call for the many *bezai-sen*, the round-hulled and

carvel-planked vessels with junk-type rigging, which carried cargo between Osaka and Edo. They could carry cargo up to 1000 *koku*, the equivalent of 5000 bushels (1 *koku* was roughly 180 liters).

The area around Tagonoura has long been known for its production of *washi*, or 'Japanese paper.' Though Japanese paper is made from a variety of materials, the *washi* from this area was made from *mitsumata*, the 'oriental paper bush.' The area was ideally situated, as the shrubs flourished on the fertile volcanic soil, while the copious amounts of clean water needed in the paper-making process came down from the volcano's slopes. Fuji's paper was not just made for local consumption, for the Tōkaidō and the port of Tagonoura made its distribution to the rest of the country easy.

Things changed dramatically in the wake of the Second World War, when the introduction of Western paper-making processes led to the area's rapid industrialization. Its attending bleaching or de-inking processes, combined with the burning of residue pulp, placed huge pressure on the environment. Where the area was once known for its pristine water, it now became one of Japan's most polluted areas, with exploding rates of lung cancer among the local population. The residue pulp also found its way into the local rivers. During the 50s and 60s, the problem grew so that the port of Taganoura was perennially clogged by a thick mass of odiously stinking sludge.

It was only later, under pressure from local environmental groups during the sixties and seventies, that things began to change. Since then, many improvements have been made, so that today the rivers are clean again. Yet the once so romantic scenery has been lost forever.

HAKONE

Ashinoko

Ashinoko or Lake Ashi has always been a scenic highlight for Japanese travelers. One of its charms is that it provides a perfect view of Mt. Fuji, without the clutter of Japan's urbanized east coast. The lake lies at a height of 723 m, just below the Hakone Pass, which lies at 846 m. The reason for its altitude is that its waters fill a so-called caldera, a cauldron-like hollow that was formed when, some three thousand years ago, the volcano of Mt. Kami erupted and collapsed in on itself.

One of the area's historic attractions is the Hakone Shrine, which lies hidden in the woods on the north-

ern shore of the lake, just a short stroll away from the tourist resort of Hakone village. The shrine is said to have been founded in 757 by a priest from Kyoto who went by the name of Mangan. He had been sent thither to galvanize the local traditions of mountain worship to the greater good of the Buddhist and Shintō temples and shrines. In those days, the two religions went hand in hand. Called *shinbutsu shūgō*, or the 'syncretism of Shintō and Buddhism,' it was a uniquely Japanese way to unite two widely diverging belief systems, in which the foreign tradition of Buddhism was made to assimilate the indigenous Shintō traditions. It was the state's approach to religion throughout Japan's history until the Meiji government reversed it toward the end of the 19th century.

An attraction that only lies in store for those who tread the paved sections that remain of the old Tōkaidō highway, is the Amazake Chaya. Sitting 2 km down the road toward Yumoto, the old thatched teahouse is better known for its *amazake*, a low-alcohol drink made from fermented rice that is served piping hot. There used to be many more such teahouses, but the opening of National Route 1 has ensured the demise of all but this one teahouse. The interior, too, is traditional: a large open

HAKONE – Ashinoko

Lake Ashi today, made unsafe
by a veritable pirate ship

fireplace with a raised floor, wooden tree stumps for seats, and a floor of compacted earth. The Amazake Chaya is the Tōkaidō's only remaining original teahouse. Only along the Nakasendō, the ancient inland highroad, can one find teahouses that still breathe the same historic atmosphere.

HAKONE – Ashinoko

Left: The Amazake Chaya today

Below: Yumoto during the early Meiji period

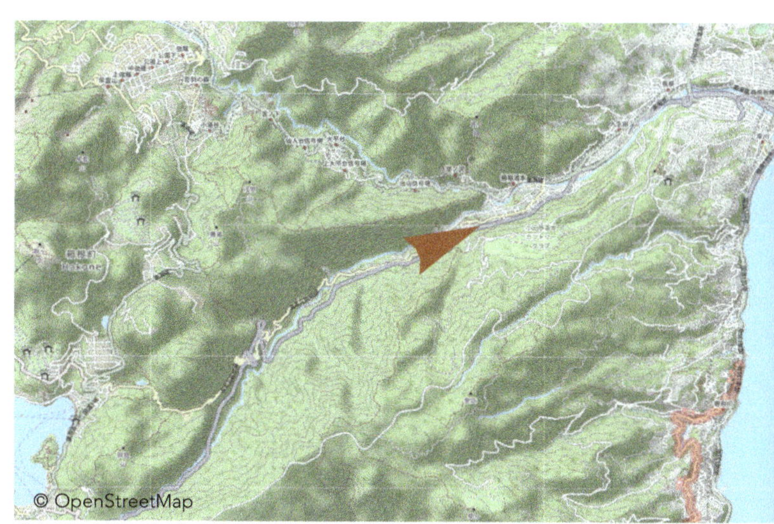

Yumoto

The small mountain village of Yumoto, tucked away among the eastern slopes of the Hakone Mountains, has long been famous for its hot springs. Yumoto's potential as a resort is said to have been discovered when a monk by the name of Shakujō Jōbō happened on a hot spring while crossing the Hakone Pass in 738. Little is known about the monk, but Yumoto is known throughout

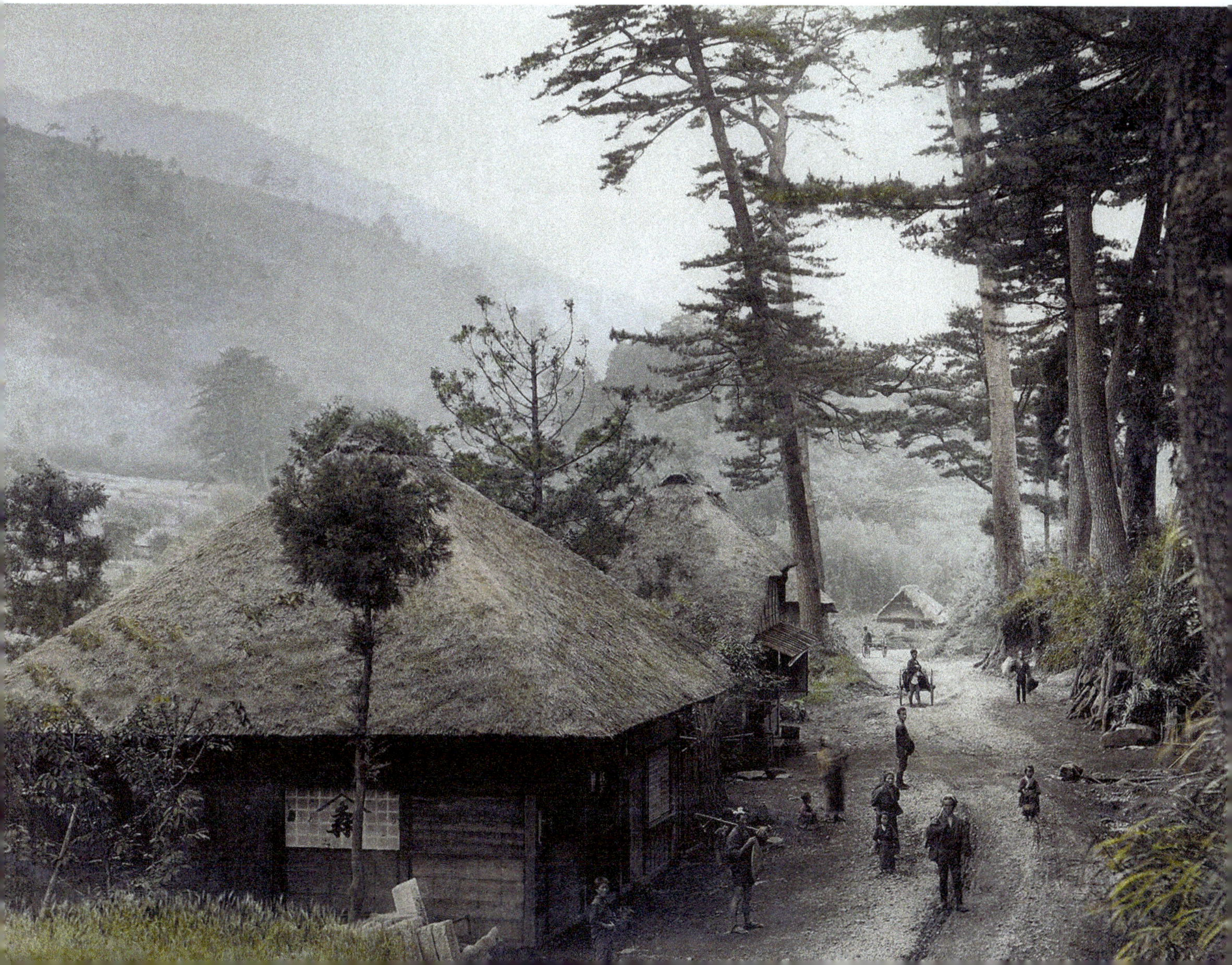

Japan. Yomoto actually means 'source of a hot spring.' and this the village has proven to be, for sixteen more onsen, or 'hot springs' have been discovered since Jōbō's lucky discovery, making Yumoto a prime destination for hot spring aficionados in the Kantō region.

One of its most illustrious visitors was the great *Taikō* Toyotomi Hideyoshi, who chose Yumoto as the place from which to conduct his epic siege against the Hōjō clan of nearby Odawara Castle. He set up his headquarters at Yumoto's Sōun Temple, the very temple that had been founded by the clan's patriarch Hōjō Sōun. It was not only to spite the Hōjō that Hideyoshi chose Yumoto; he too was attracted by its hot springs and spent much of his time between war councils indulging in lavish parties that started out on the temple grounds and ended up with long soaks in one of Yumoto's hot springs. He had his whole ménage brought over from his headquarters of Nagahama Castle on the east shore of Lake Biwa and invited over cronies from the capital to entertain them as they sat out the long wait for Odawara Castle to finally fall. They weren't ruffians either. Far from it. Among them were cultured men like Hon-inbō Sansa, one of the country's best Go players. Another celebrity was Hon'ami Kōetsu, a man who started out as a sword polisher but climbed the feudal social ladder through his mastery in other fields like calligraphy and painting. Most famous among them was the tea master Sen no Rikyū, who had not yet fallen out of favor with the *taikō* and was called upon to prepare him and his guest tea at the Sōun Temple.

Yumoto became so popular as a tourist destination that, when in 1888, a group of Odawara indus-trialists took up the initiative to build a horse tramway that would connect their city to the important hub of Kōzu Railway Station along the Tōkaidō Main Line, they made Yumoto the tram line's westernmost terminal. The line, which was completed by the end of the year, was Japan's third horse tramway, covered a stretch of 12,7 km, and reached a height of 96 m. As can be imagined, the horses that had to pull the tram uphill had a hard task, especially in Japan's hot summers, so that, by the turn of the century, **the tram line was electrified**.

Since then, the tram line has been converted into a full-fledged mountain line (the Hakone Tozan Tsusudō), which connects Odawara to Sōunzan Station, high up in the Hakone Mountains. There one can mount a cable car on the Hakone Ropeway, to the northern shore of Lake Ashi, where one can board a modern-day pirate ship that crosses the lake toward Hakone village on the southern end of the lake.

HAKONE – Yumoto

ODAWARA

Tōkaidō

When Felice Beato visited Odawara in the 1870s, he did not set up his camera on the grounds of Odawara Castle but along the Tōkaidō. He was, after all, recording the ancient highroad in the same way as Utagawa Hiroshige had done in his famed woodblock prints. Beato did so just east of the Hakone-*guchi* Intersection, near what today is the castle's southern entrance. In those days, the castle grounds extended farther southward; the

Kōen Temple

castle's southern moat ran parallel with the Tōkaidō, just behind the row of houses that lined the high road on the right-hand side.

The wooded hill in the distance, too, was part of the castle grounds. It formed the southern reach of Mt. Hachiman, on whose eastern slope the castle was situated. Toward the southern side of the slope, just within the Itabashi-*guchi*, the town's western gate, lay the grounds of the Kōen and Gyokuden temples. Just above the sloping top of a roof on the lefthand side of Beato's photograph one can make out the top of an ancient **ginkgo tree**, which still marks the grounds of the **Kōen Temple**.

Below: Enoshima during the early Meiji period photographed by Kusakabe Mimbei

Right: The Iwaya Caves during the early 20th century

KAMAKURA

Enoshima

The island of Eno ('shima' means island) features largely in Japanese history, part of the reason being that it lay so close to Kamakura, which was the center of feudal power during the period to which it lent its name. Its mythical history goes back in

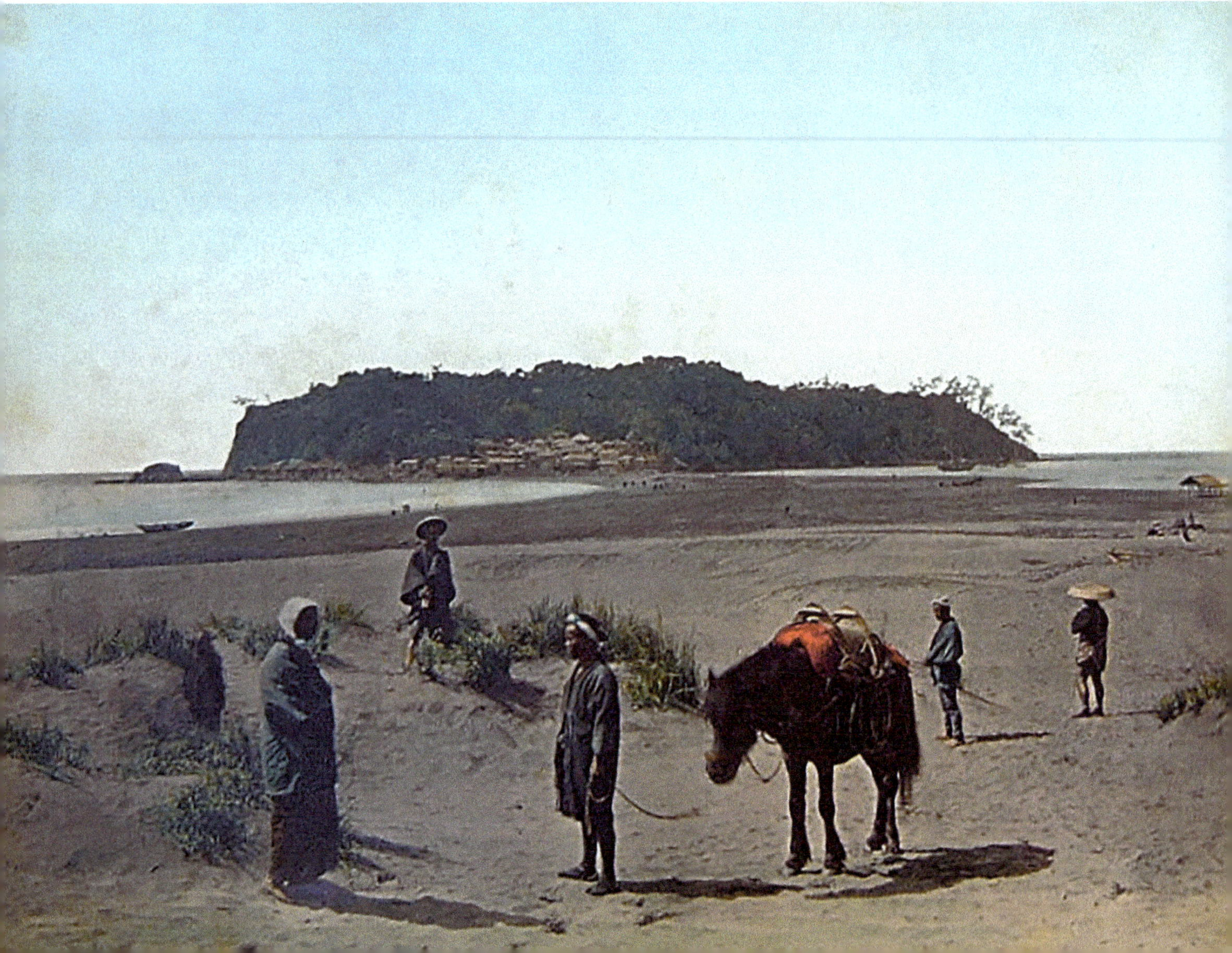

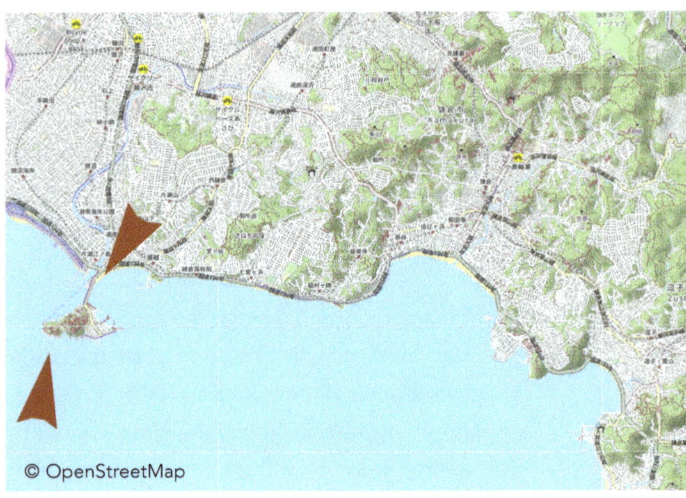

time much further. Part of that history was written by the resident Chinese monk Kōkei (977–1049), who wrote a history of the island's temples and shrines called the *Enoshima engi*. It relates how a five-headed dragon terrorized the simple fisherfolk along the coast until Benzaiten, the Goddess of Eloquence, caused the island to emerge from the bay to provide a dwelling for the monster. Initially, samurai and monks venerated Benzaiten in a complex of caves on the west tip of the island. Later, the locals built the Enoshima Shrine, which is dedicated to the goddess.

The area around Enoshima has changed drastically since the Meiji period, when old photographs show a beach as yet unspoiled by concrete, steel, or tarmac. Today, the National Highway Route 134 skirts the beach atop a concrete sea wall. Behind it, Enoshima's high-rise apartment blocks with a view of the island stand shoulder to shoulder. Access to the island itself has also 'improved' with the Enoshima Ōhashi, not yet the kind of suspension bridge to Awaji Island near Akashi, but already made out of solid concrete.

Today, one can take a tour of the Iwaya Caves by descending a long flight of stairs through a tunnel leading down from the shrine to the largest cave. The cave branches out toward the sea in two directions. Exiting the cave toward the east, one emerges on a raised concrete pathway leading to the other cave. Exiting the cave toward the west, another concrete pathway around the headland leads toward a pier from where one can take a ferry to the foot of the Benten-*bashi*, the bridge that connects the historic island to the mainland. In total, the caves extend over a distance of more than two hundred meters.

Tsurugaoka Hachiman-gū

Being not far removed from Yokohama's foreign
settlement, Enoshima and Kamakura's other many
attractions were a favorite destination for its settlers,
tourists, and resident photographers alike. Situated
just twenty kilometers away, on the opposite side
of the Miura Peninsula, one could easily travel
down to Kamakura on horseback or by *rikisha* in
a day, as well as do the sights. Not surprisingly,
images of Kamakura during the early Meiji period
abound. One of Yokohama's foreign photographers
to visit and photograph Kamakura was the Austrian
Baron Raimund von Stillfried.

One of Kamakura's main attractions was and is the Tsurugaoka Hachiman-*gū*. Built in 1063, the shrine's original site was at Yui no Wakamiya (present-day Zaimoku), overlooking Sagami Bay. Back then, it was called the Tsurugaoka Wakamiya. It was the great Minamoto no Yoritomo, who, on the eve of his epic war with the Taira, decided to move the shrine-cum-temple to its present location. By then, his ancestor Yoshiie had already given it the name by which it is known today. Several times throughout its long history, the shrine has been damaged or destroyed by fire, most notably in 1526, when it was set ablaze by Satomi forces in their siege of Kamakura.

Incredibly, the most recent act of arson was perpetrated on behalf of the Meiji government, which, in 1870, as part of its *shinbutsu bunri* policy, ordered all of the shrine's Buddhist-related buildings to be destroyed. Much of their interiors, too, was lost, sold off to foreigners and shipped abroad. The two giant wooden wardens (*niō*) that guarded the entrance were spared but had to be moved to the main hall of the nearby Jūfuku Temple, where they still reside today.

The Tsurugaoka Hachiman-*gū*'s today

Raimund von Stillfried (1839–1911) was the son of Baron August Wilhelm Stillfried von Rathenitz and Countess Maria Anna Johanna Theresia Walburge Clam-Martinitz. Though trained as a military man, Von Stillfried left the army early on in his career to travel the world. He initially went to South America, from where he traveled on to China and eventually Japan, arriving in Yokohama in 1864. He initially became an assistant at the Legation of the North German Federation. It seems that, by then, he was already an accomplished photographer, although it is widely assumed that he honed his craft under his fellow settler-photographer Felice Beato. Von Stillfried opened his own studio in 1871 and named it Stillfried & Co. Four years later, he teamed up with the German photographer Hermann Andersen, and the name of the studio was changed to Stillfried & Andersen, though it also was known as the Japan Photographic Association. The next few years were some of Von Stillfried's most productive. In 1876, he sold much of his collection to Kusakabe Kimbei, who then still worked for Felice Beato, though he became Von Stillfried's protégé when, a year later, Stillfried & Andersen acquired Beato's studio and much of its stock. When, in 1878, the partnership between Von Stillfried and Andersen was dissolved, Andersen continued to operate their studio under the same name until, in 1885, it was acquired by Adolfo Farsari. By then, Von Stillfried had

already quit Japan to return to Vienna, where he settled as a photographer by appointment to the imperial court.

Kamakura Daibutsu

Another resident photographer from Yokohama was Suzuki Shinichi, who had learned his craft under Shimooka Renjō and operated a photographic portrait studio on the settlement's Benten-*dōri*.

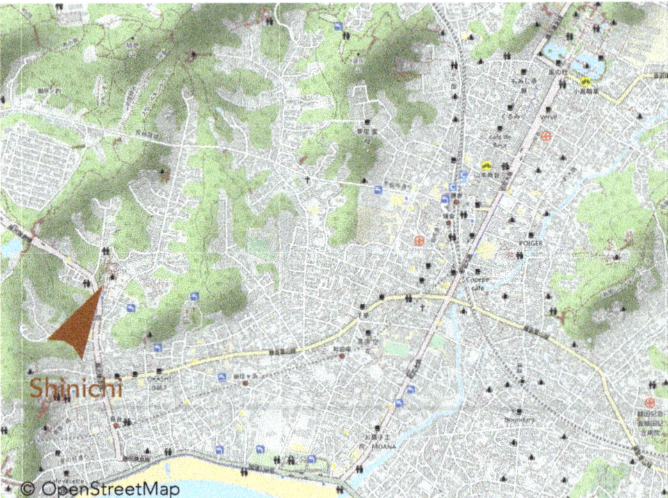

Shinichi, too, made grateful use of Kamakura's proximity. And what better way than to photograph the Kamakura's Daibutsu, the great bronze statue of Buddha that sits on the grounds of the Kōtoku-*in*, a Buddhist temple on the western outskirts of the temple town.

The original statue was made out of wood. Work on the wooden statue began in 1238 under the direction of a Buddhist priest by the name of Jōkō. It was completed in 1243, when Jōkō held a ceremony to consecrate the Buddha. Like the Great Buddha Statue of Nara's Tōdai Temple, the statue was housed in a huge hall called the Daibutsu-*den*. When, just five years later, a typhoon destroyed the hall and severely damaged the statue, work was begun to cast the bronze that still causes visitors to catch their breath today.

Suzuki Shinichi (1835–1918) started out in life as Takahashi Shinichi. His family lived in a small village on the Itō Peninsula. At the age of twenty, he married into the Suzuki family from Shimoda and took on the family name. The Suzuki made their living from wickerwork. But when, in 1867, a tsunami destroyed the business, he moved to Yokohama to begin an apprenticeship at the photographic studio of Shimooka Renjō (1823–1914), a man who is widely considered to be Japan's first professional photographer. Six years later, Shinichi set up his own studio specializing in portraits and souvenir albums. In 1878, he opened up a branch office in Tokyo's Kudanzaka, and in 1889, he was commissioned to make the official portrait of Emperor Meiji and his consort. Shinichi's greatest contribution to the promotion of the art of photography in Japan came in 1902,

when he founded the Joshi Shashin Denshū-sho, Japan's first academy to teach the art of photography to female students.

YOKOHAMA

Kyoryūchi

The foreign settlement of Yokohama was established shortly after Japan and the United States ratified the Treaty of Amity and Commerce in 1858. The treaty envisioned nearby Kanagawa to be opened up to foreign trade. But the waters in front

of Kanagawa were shallow and situated right along the Tōkaidō, it was feared that foreigners might be

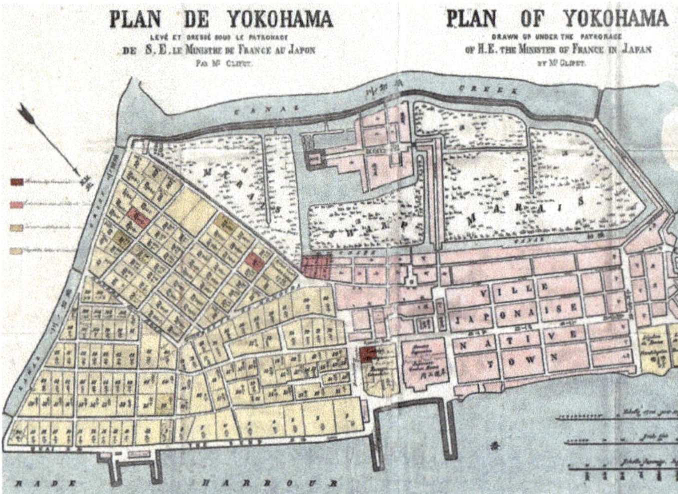

targeted by nationalists who were against what they considered an 'unequal treaty.' That such fears were well grounded was borne out by a string of attacks on foreigners over the next decades. And thus the *bakufu* chose Yokohama instead. Compared to Kanagawa, it had several advantages: it had deeper waters, it was situated well away from the Tōkaidō, and it was as yet largely undeveloped. To further enhance the safety of its foreign settlers, a wide moat was dug to create an artificial island. The Japanese called it the Horikiri-*gawa*; the foreigners just referred to it as the Canal.

The first structures to arise along its dirt roads laid out in a checkered pattern were mostly in the Japanese tradition, though not all of the area within the canal was at first fully developed. On its north side lay what was known as The Swamp, a barren piece of flatland. Within the Swamp sat another, smaller island occupied by a number of rickety buildings known as the **Yomizaki Yūkaku**. It was

the settlement's red-light district, populated by
prostitutes recruited from Edo's vast Yoshiwara red-

light district, which lay well outside the Treaty
Limits. It was also known as the **Gankirō**, after the
area's main brothel, which in turn was named after
its owner, Gankiya Sakichi. Besides brothels, the

known as the Butaya or Pig Shop. It probably
served deep-fried pork, for on one fateful morning,
on 26 November 1866, its cook upset his stove,
causing the oil to catch on fire. The **Great Butaya
Fire** spread through the Gankirō, killing some four
hundred of its occupants. Fanned on by a brisk

area also contained a theater, some teahouses,
and various restaurants. One of them was a joint

off-land wind, the fire spread to **Honmachi-*dōri***,
until most of the settlement was reduced to ashes.

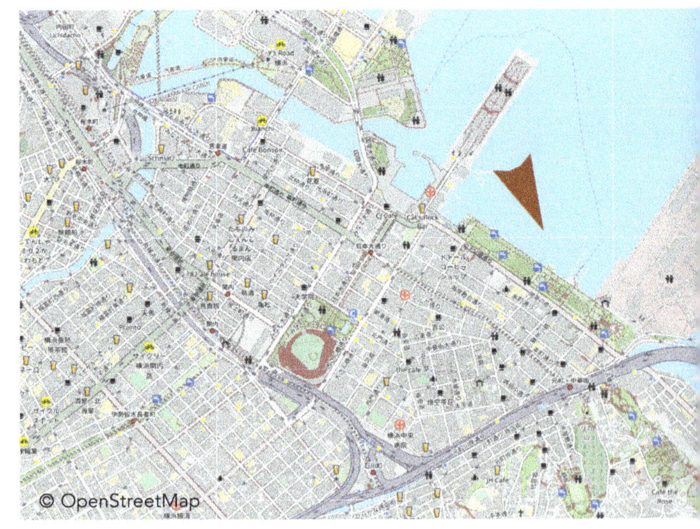

The Bund

A far more 'respectable' part of town was The Bund. As at Kobe, it was the wide boulevard along the seafront, with a wonderful view of the fleet of foreign ships moored on Yokohama's pier. It was the place where Yokohama's most prestigious companies, such as Aspinall, Mackenzie & Co. (No. 9) and the Netherlands Trading Society (No 5), had set up their offices in grand, colonial-style buildings, right alongside the Club Hotel (No. 5b) and the Dutch consulate (also No. 5).

At The Bund's east end, and at the settlement's center, lay Yokohama's pier. There were two piers, in fact, creating a harbor where foreign ships could moor and unload their cargo. The Japanese customs officers whose task it was to inspect the cargo

YOKOHAMA – The Bund

Left: The Bund and The Bluff
during the 1890s

Below: Yokohama's piers and Customs
House at the turn of the century

were housed in a large building right in front of the piers. Most of the foreign consulates, too, were situated here, in a separate building that stood next to the customs house. The latter marked the line of separation between the foreign quarter on the west and the native quarter on the east.

Benten- and Honmura-dōri

Much of the original settlement of Yokohama that can be seen in the photographs on the previous pages was destroyed by the Butaya Fire of 1866. In its wake arose a new town. It was populated by modern, brick-and-mortar buildings in the image of those found in Western capitals.

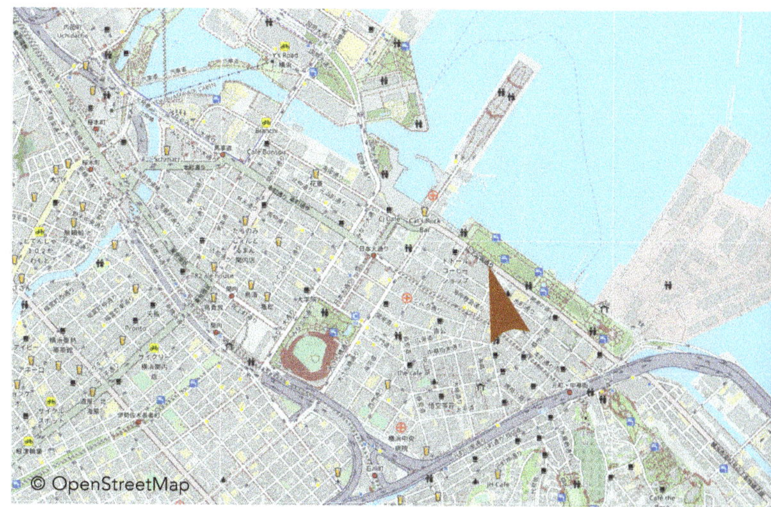

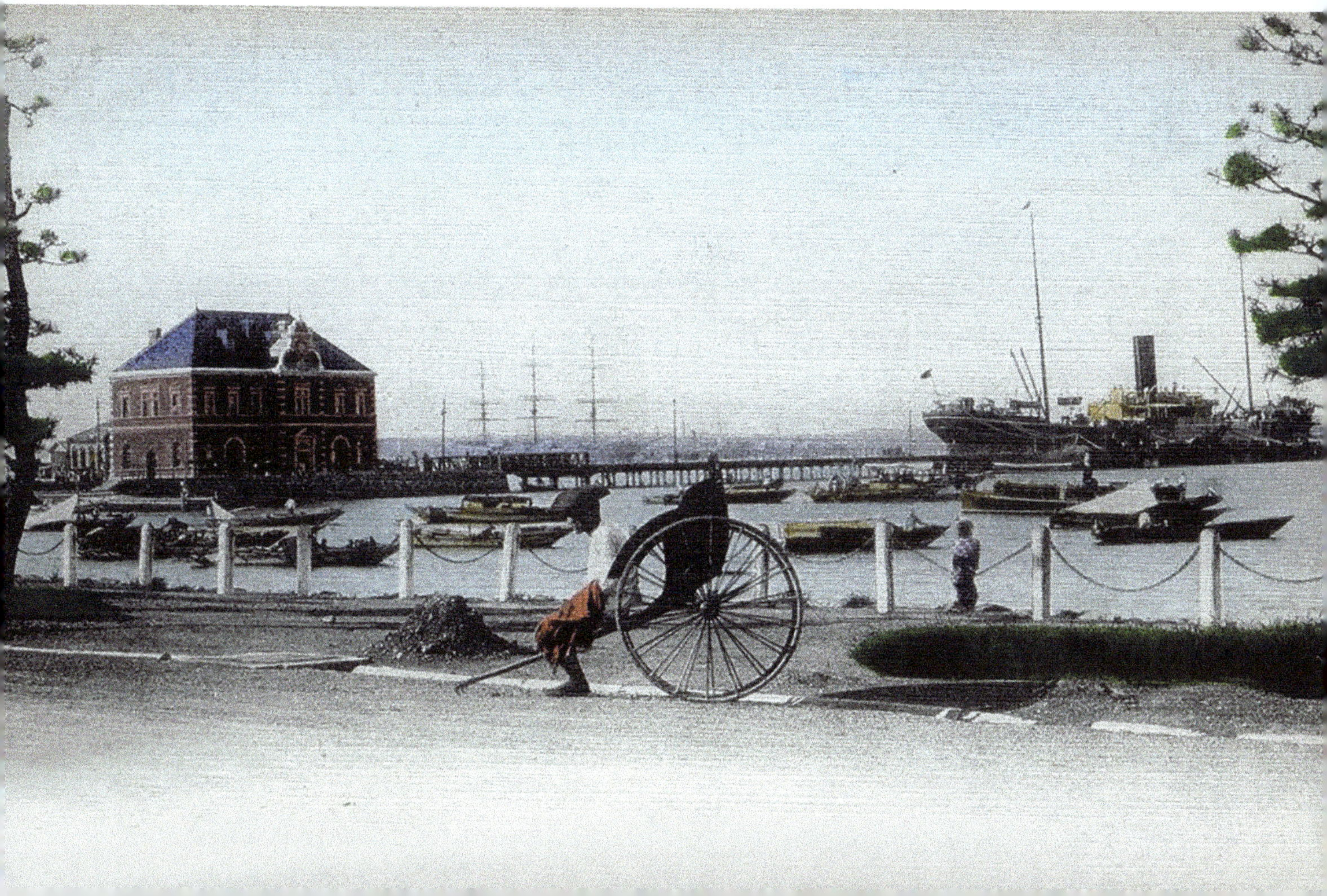

The *Hikawa-maru* moored in front of
what is now Yamashita Park

HOTEL NEW GRAND

Below: Looking westward along Homura Road toward the Bluff around the turn of the century

Right: The 100 Steps leading up The Bluff during the early Meiji period

The main road through the native quarter was Benten-*dōri*. It was the road where all the Japanese and Chinese curiosity shops could be found, as well as the studios of Yokohama's resident foreign and native photographers.

The main road through Yokohama's foreign quarter (today's Chinatown) was Honmura-*dōri*, which started out at the northeast corner of the Swamp and ran due east to the heart of the quarter to make a right angle southwards toward The Bluff.

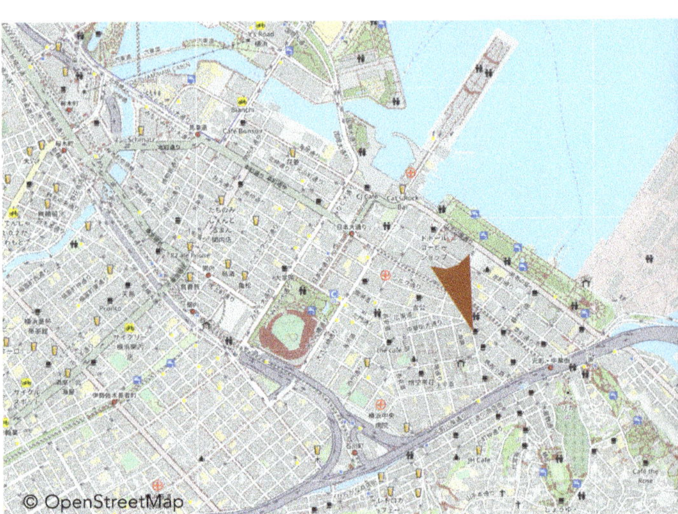

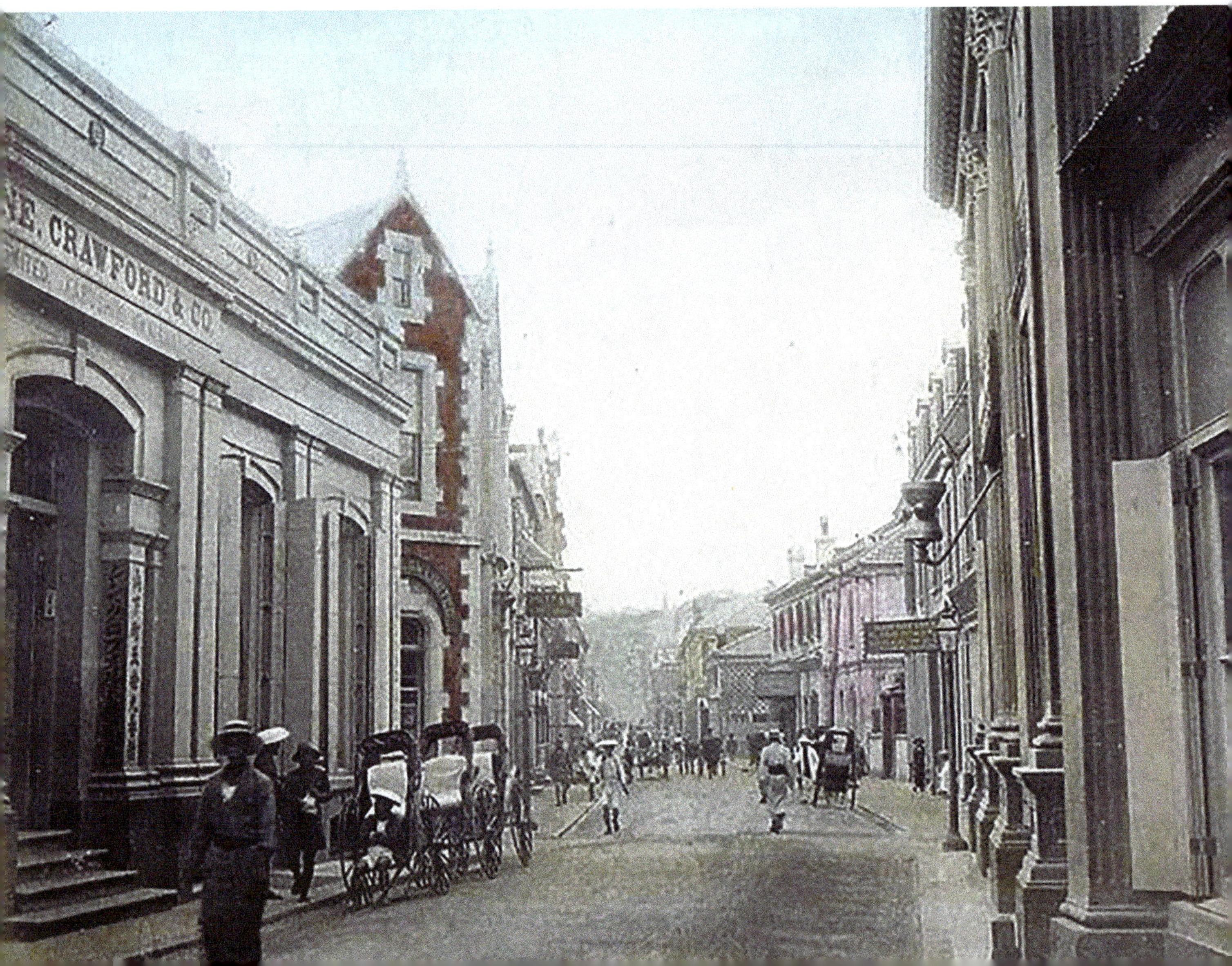

The Bluff

At the end of Honmura-*dōri*, in the western corner of the artificial island that was Yokohama, just next to the British Legation, one could cross the Maeda Brdige bridge across the Horibō Canal. This would bring one to a part of town called Moto-*machi*. Moto-*machi* lay at the foot of The Bluff, a small headland from which one got a beautiful view of the settlement and the ships riding at their anchors. Its crest could be reached by treading a stone stairway called The 100 Steps. It was a favorite spot to enjoy Sunday picnics, or what the colonial British in those days referred to as 'going for tiffin.'

It was Commodore Matthew Calbraith Perry who gave The Bluff its name. On 8 March 1854, 'a fine day, not overmuch cold,' he landed at Yokohama to negotiate the terms of the Treaty of Peace and Amity. There, at a site that is now known as the Port Opening Square at the city's heart, the *bakufu* had prepared a hastily erected building for both parties to meet. Two weeks earlier, on the evening of 24 February, he was rounding the headland aboard the flagship USS *Powhatan* to cast anchor off Kanagawa, when he is said to have remarked on the cliffs. Lit up orange in the descending winter sun, they appeared to him like a 'Mandarin Bluff.'

YOKOHAMA – The Bluff

Left: View of Yokohama from the Bluff at the turn of the century

Below: Honmoku photographed by Kusakabe Kimbei, with in the foreground the hamlet of Negishi

Honmoku

On the opposite side of The Bluff, just around the headland, lay Honmoku, a stretch of Dover-like cliffs crested with pine trees. At their feet lay wide sandy flats that ran for miles when the tide was out. Once they had been the place from where the powerful Hōjō clan launched their fleet of warships to do battle with the Satomi from across the bay. Yet it had always been a place where local fishermen drew their *beka-bune* onto the flat sands to unload their catch of the day and the place where their womenfolk harvested kelp and clams.

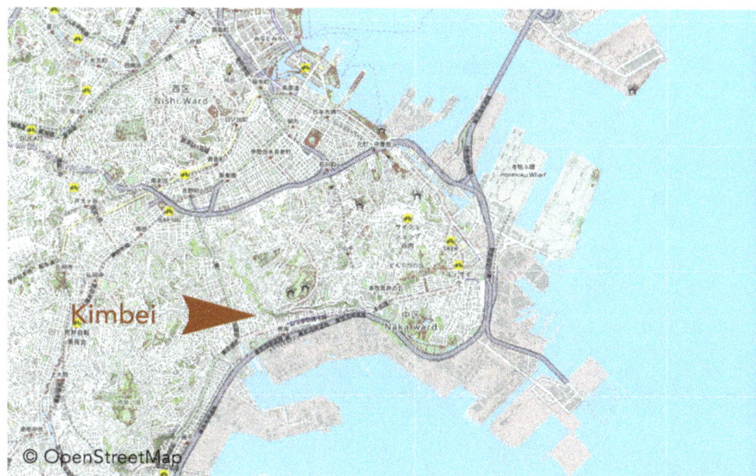

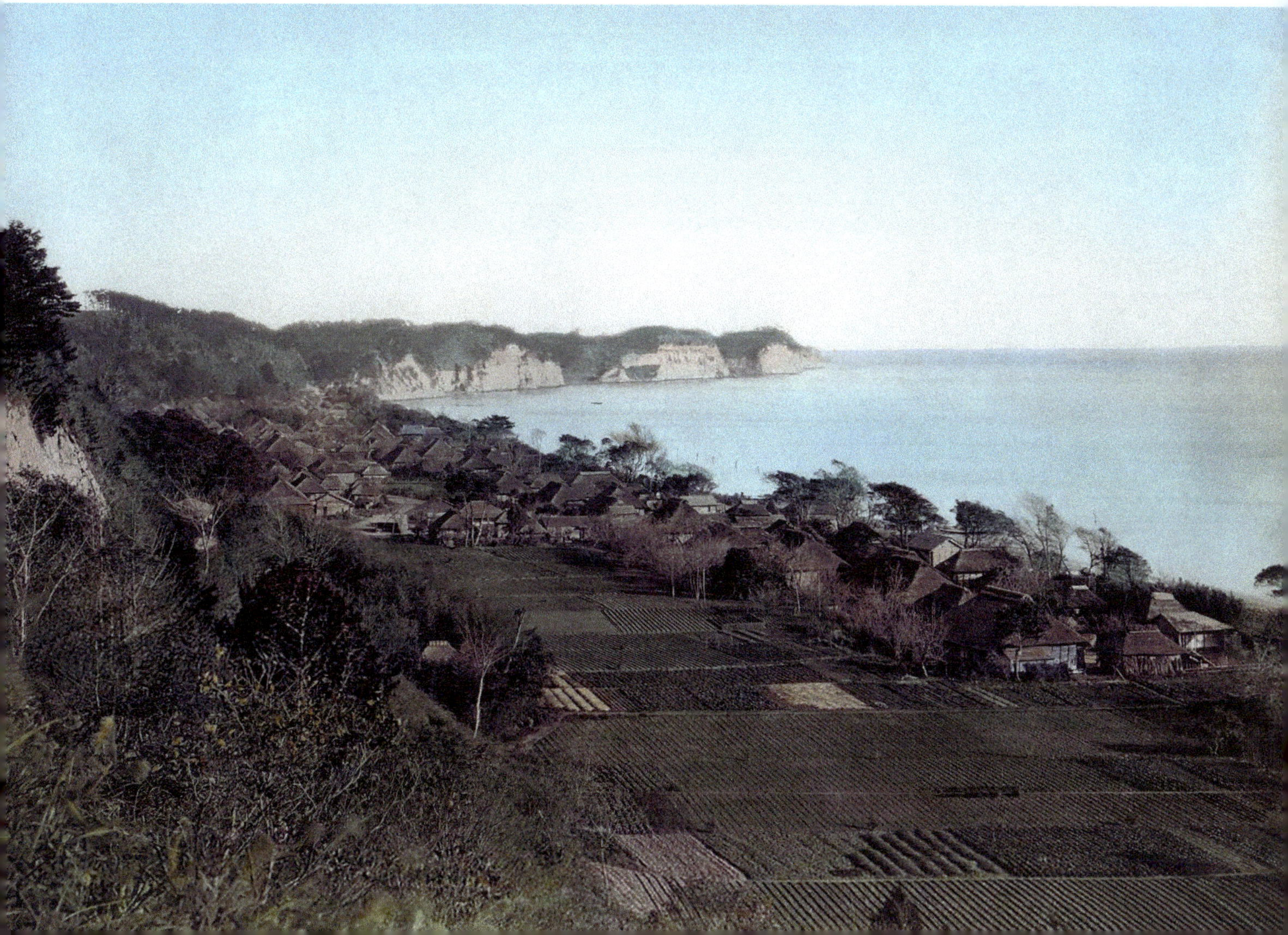

Below: Honmoku around 1890, photographed by Kusakabe Kimbei

Right: Honmoku Jūniten during the Meiji period, today the site of a sewage treatment plant

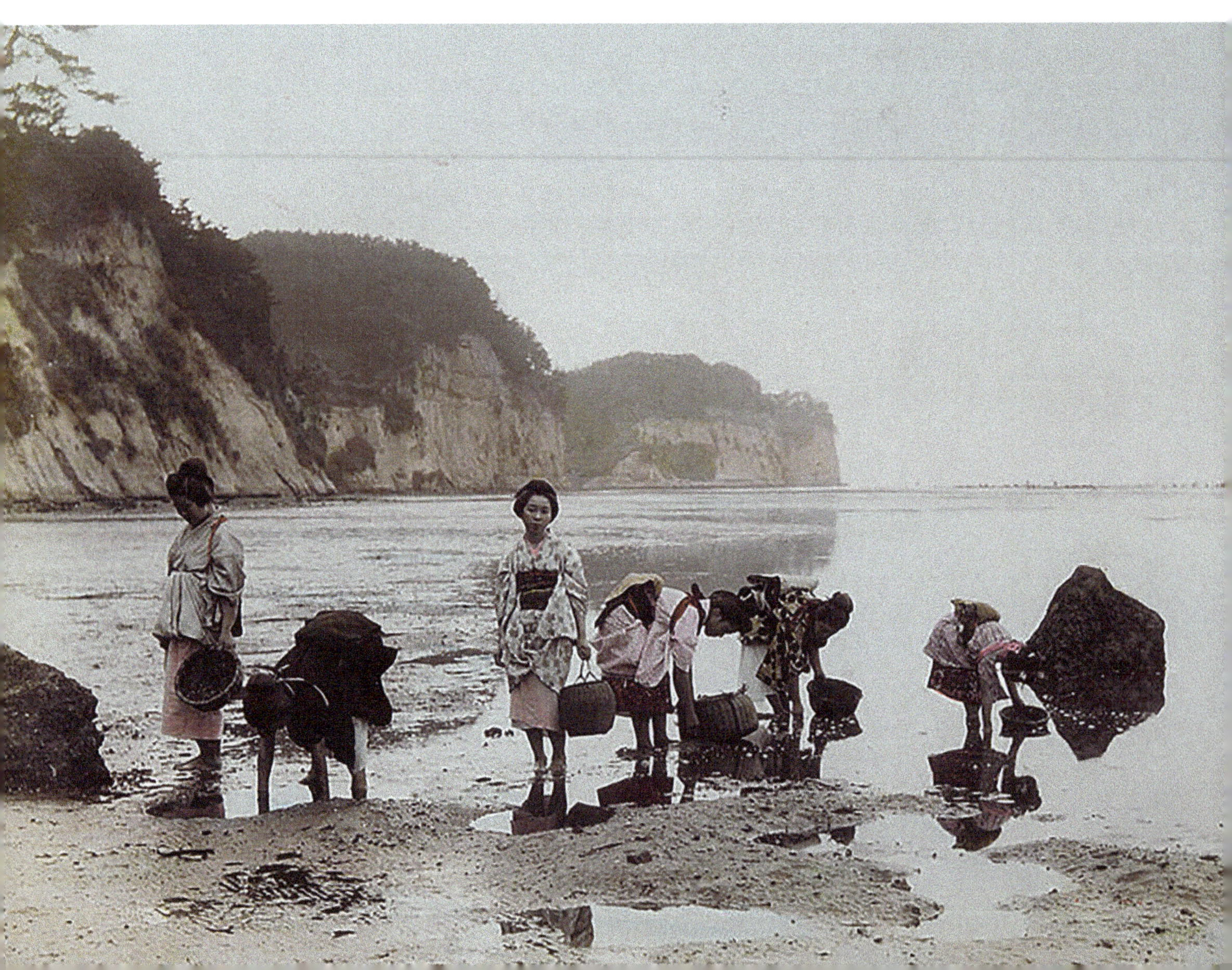

During the Meiji period, Honmoku had become somewhat of a seaside resort. One of its attractions was the Sankei-*en*, Japanese-style gardens with ponds, streams, and narrow paths nestled among the cliffs. It was financed and designed by Hara Tomitarō, a wealthy local silk merchant who used his fortune to collect art and tea utensils. The garden was partly meant to provide the perfect setting for tea ceremonies. For this, he also began collecting historic buildings from around the country

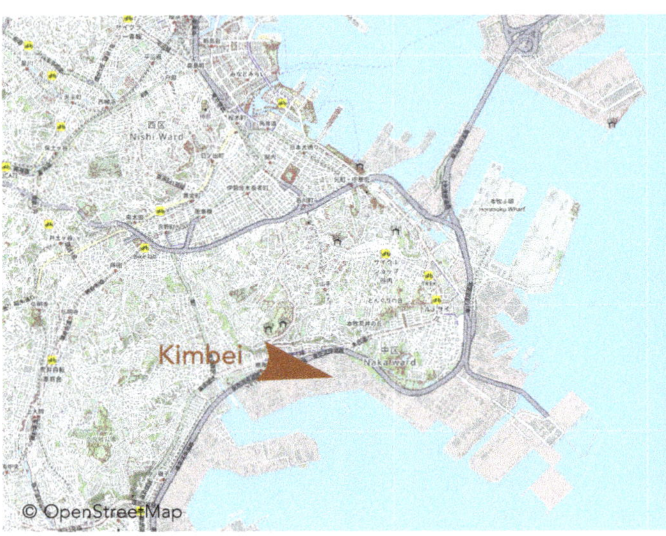

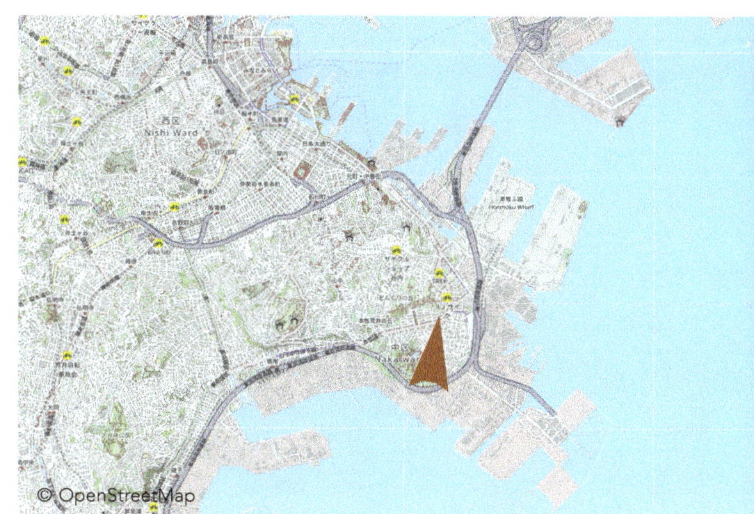

that were in danger of being lost. The first such structure was the Jutō Ōi-*dō* from Kyoto's Tenzui Temple, which was built in 1591 by Toyotomi Hideyoshi as a resting place for his mother. Then came the Rinshu-*kaku*, a summer residence that used to grace the grounds of the Wakayama estate of the Kii House of Tokugawa and dates back to the middle of the 17th century. They were followed by the Gekka-*den* and the Sunsō-*ro*, two structures from Uji's Mimuroto Temple. Tomitarō went on to collect a total of twelve structures, ten of which are now Important Cultural Properties. The gardens were opened to the public in 1906.

YOKOHAMA – Honmoku

It was the brick-and-mortar that eventually would prove fatal to many of Yokohama's dwellers when, on 1 September 1923, the region was devastated by the Great Kantō Earthquake. Again Yokohama was rebuilt, and again it was destroyed when, on 29 May 1945, 517 Allied B-29 Super Fortresses dropped 2570 tons of incendiary bombs over the industrial port city.

As in so many other places, Yokohama has undergone profound changes during the post-war decades. The Canal that separated the one-time settlement from the mainland was filled in. Over it arose the elevated tracks of the Keihin Tōhoku and Negishi lines, and where once ran water, cars now dive into tunnels to emerge on the other side of town. Near Kannai Station, where once stood the Gankirō, now towers Yokohama Stadium, home to the Yokohama DeNA BayStars and the venue for concerts by the world's leading pop acts.

Like Yokohama, Honmoku, too, has changed. In 1959, at the end of the Allied occupation, plans were drawn up to turn the coastline into an indus-trial site. For that to happen, large stretches of the bay in front of the cliffs had to be reclaimed. There was much resistance from local fishermen, who argued that, due to unique local sea currents, the area was a special breeding ground for fish and fowl. But, as elsewhere, progress beckoned and the plan went ahead anyway. A decade later, the area had changed beyond recognition. Where once, the sea lapped at the feet of the cliffs, now rows and rows of huge steel silos of the ENEOS Negishi Refinery obscure the view. The cliffs remain, as well as Hara Tomitarō's Sankei-*en*. They now sit within Honmoku Shimin Park, its grounds hemmed in by the Shuto Expressway Bayshore Route. Known in Japan as the Shuto Kōsoku Wangan-*sen*, the expressway that skirts the west side of Tokyo Bay all the way to Chiba, gained worldwide notoriety during the 1990s, when it became the hunting grounds of Japanese street racing clubs. Sponsored by tuning companies like Top Secret, they used the new expressway to test-run heavily tuned cars that reached speeds of well over 300 km/h.

Left: Honmoku today, hemmed in by the Shuto Expressway Bayshore Route

TOKYO (EDO)

Atago-yama

The Edo equivalent of Yokohama's Bluff was Atago-*yama*. Unlike The Bluff, Atago-*yama* did not sit along the shore of Edo Bay but roughly a kilometer inland, right at the heart of Tokyo's Minato District). Stretching from Kanni Avenue to the northern perimeter of Shiba Park, the hill—at just 26 meters it is just that—is home to the Atago-*jinja*, a shrine that dates back to the early Edo period. Like The

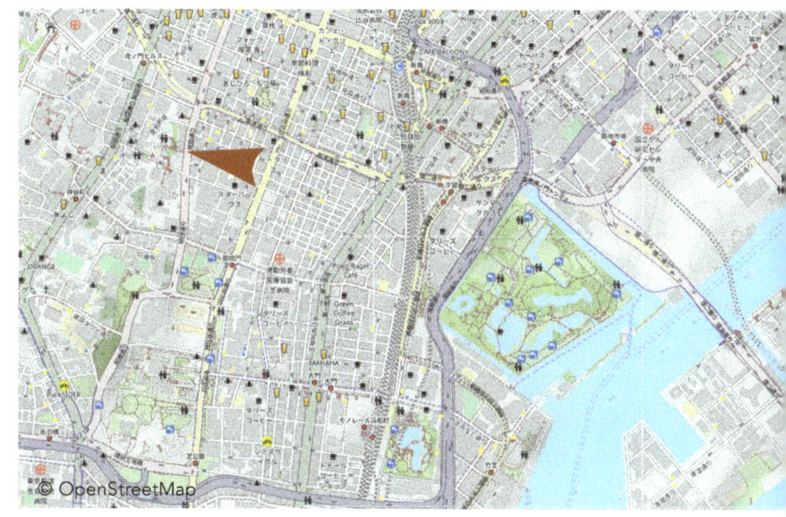

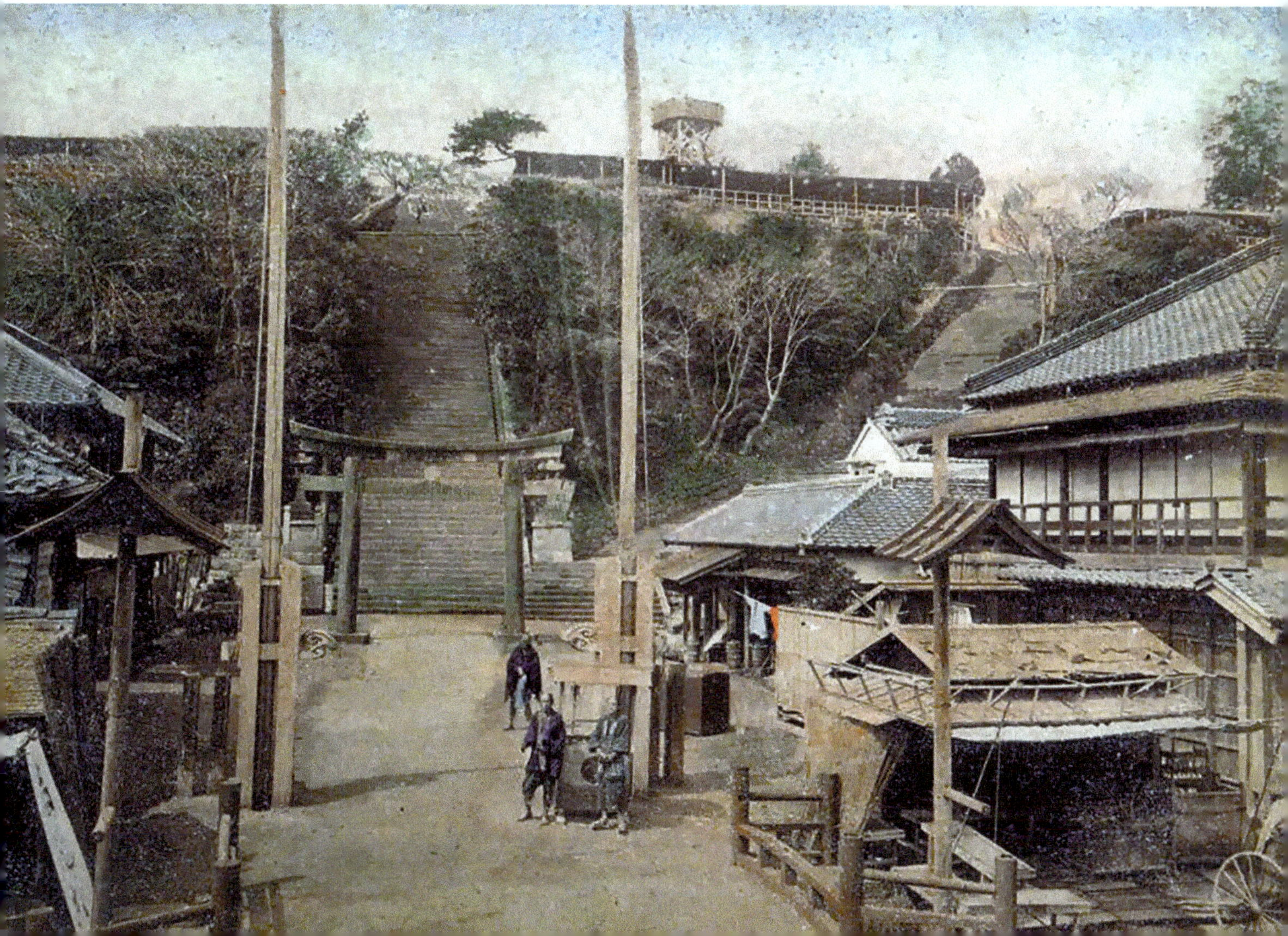

Bluff, Atago-*yama*, too, had (and still has) the proverbial 100 steps leading up to its crest and giving access to the shrine. 'Today, Mt. Atago' is dwarfed by the district's many newly arising high-rise buildings, which compete with each other in height but as yet fail to outdo nearby Tokyo Tower.

The panoramic photograph (top), taken by Felice Beato in 1865, shows a part of Edo as it had been for most of the Edo period. As such, it contrasts sharply with a similar panoramic photograph (below) that was taken from roughly the same vantage point only three decades later.

Dominating the foreground of Beato's image is the huge compound of the Edo-*hantei*, or the 'Edo residence' of the Echigo Nagaoka domain of the Makino clan. The compound was only the spare residence (*naka-yashiki*). Like other great clans, the Makino had a cluster of residences scattered around Edo, their main residence being situated at Nishinotsubo (Azabudai), with two suburban residences located at Yakushidōmai (Nihonbashi-Kodenma) and at Shibuya.

In those days, the area was still known as the Shiba district, after the Shiba Tōshōgū, a shrine dedicated to the spirit of Tokugawa Ieyasu that sits on the grounds of Shiba Park. It was founded when, in 1601, Ieyasu chose the site as the location for a statue he had commissioned to celebrate his approaching sixtieth birthday. There are many such shrines throughout Japan (at one stage there were more than five hundred!), the most famous being the Tōshōgū among the forests on the western outskirts of northern Nikkō. In Beato's photograph, the grounds of the shrine are just visible on the extreme right hand. Beyond them, one can see the shimmering surface of Edo Bay.

Hama-goten

Just right of center in boths panoramas, in the not-too-far distance, one can see the wooded grounds of the Hama-*goten*, or the 'Beach Palace' of Edo Castle. It stood on a section of reclaimed land at the head of Edo Bay. When Ieyasu took up residence, in 1590, Edo Castle had been a modest

Looking eastward over Tokyo's
Minato District from Tokyo Tower

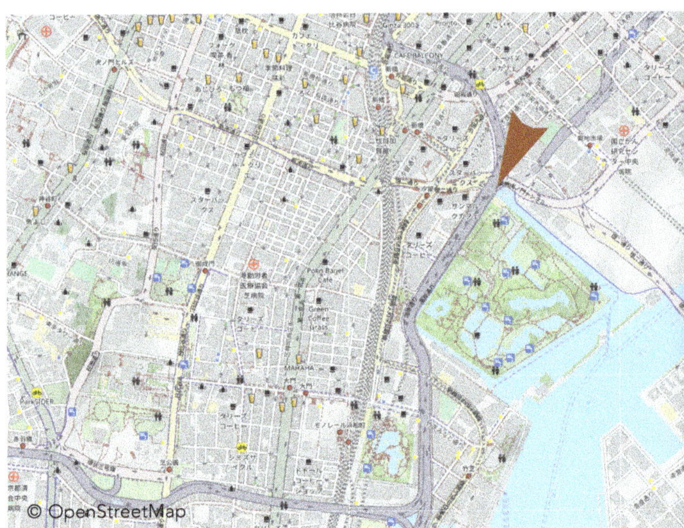

Below: The Hama-*goten* photographed from the Ōtemon-*bashi*, its northwest point of access in 1876

Right: Edo map from 1632

stronghold, and the bayside castle town provided ample room to house his retainers. With the founding of the Tokugawa *bakufu* and the massive expansion of Edo Castle, in 1603, his town planners soon ran out of space to house his retainers, and soon work began on reclaiming the shallow parts of Edo Bay in front of the castle town. The soil to fill in the reclaimed sections was taken from Kanda Hill, a stretch of elevated ground along the south bank of the Kanda River (near today's Ochanomizu Station). It resulted in the birth of well-known districts like Nihonbashi, Kyōbashi, and Ginza. To

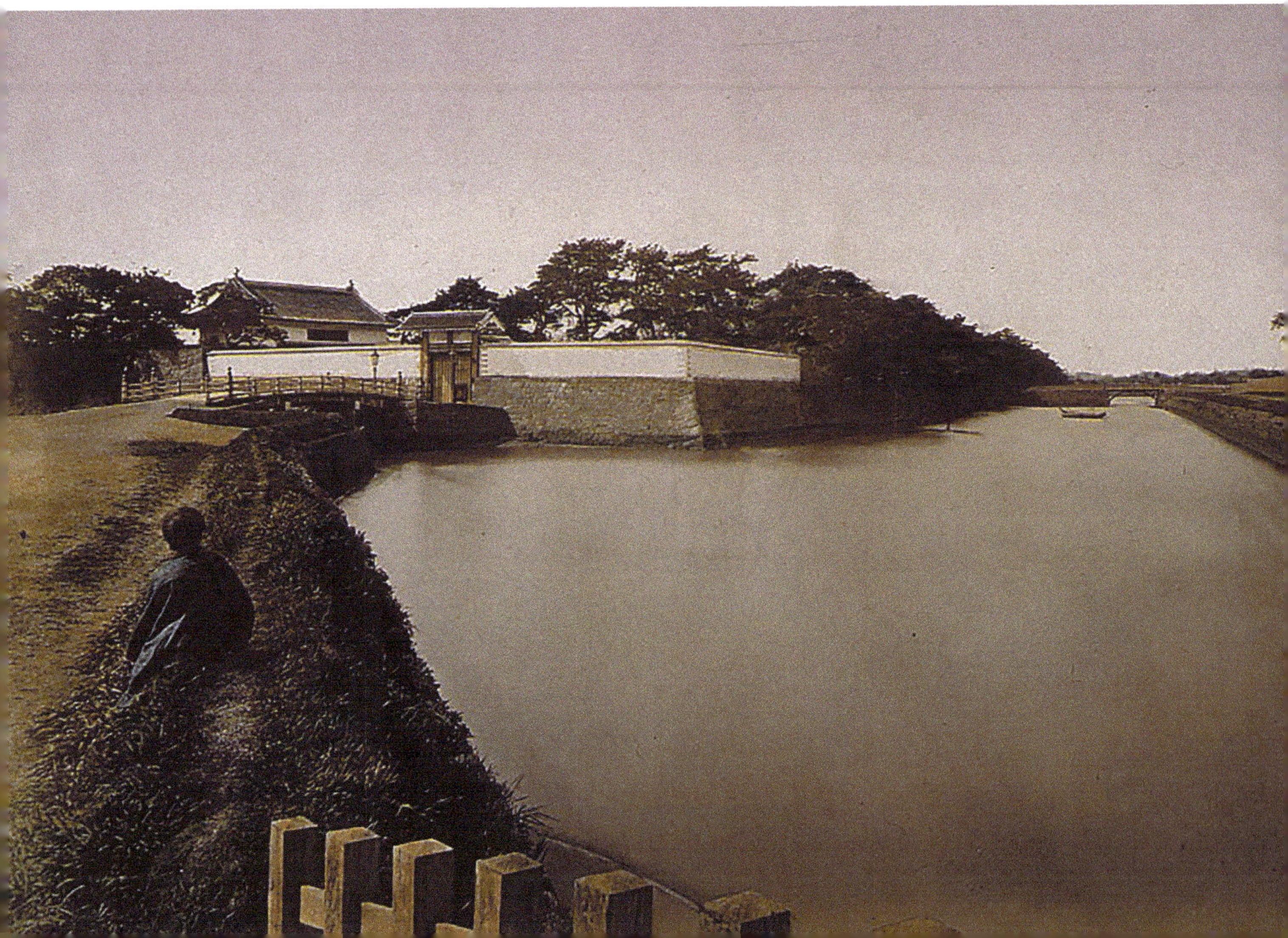

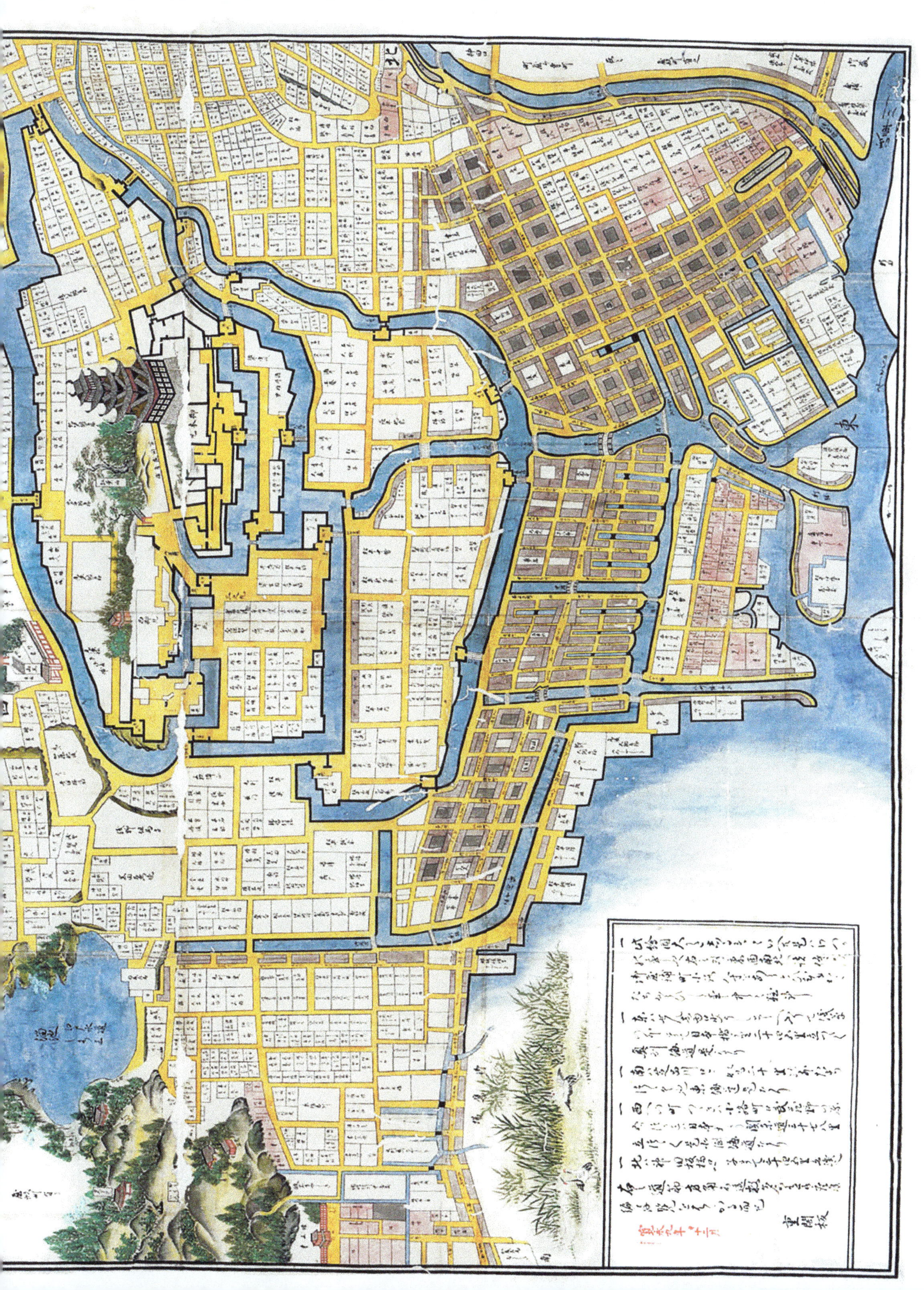

access these newly added areas the bridges of Nihon-*bashi* and Kyō-*bashi* were built. As can be seen on the map of Edo from 1632, the head of Edo Bay due east of Atago-*yama* (bottom center) had not yet been reclaimed. At that time, the Tōkaidō formed the easternmost limits of that part of the castle town, skirting wetlands toward the bay where reeds grew rampant and birds found sanctuary. Those wetlands were a favorite hunting ground of Ieysu, whose great pastime was falconry. Ieyasu passed his passion on to his offspring, including Tokugawa Tsunashige, the younger brother of the third *shōgun* Iemitsu. Tsunashige's domain lay near Kōfu, but when, in 1654, he was allowed to reclaim land at his grandfather's hunting grounds, he took to the project with relish. Appointing two of his retainers as construction magistrates, he had them build a large summer residence with vast gardens to practice his grandfather's pastime. One of the garden's features was a miniature island that changed its shape with the ebb and flow of Edo Bay. Another was a man-made hill from which to view Mt. Fuji.

When, in 1709, Tsunashige's son, Ienobu, became the 6th Tokugawa *shōgun*, the Hama-*goten* only gained importance. Two years earlier, the childless 5th *shōgun*, Tsunayoshi, had already erected a number of teahouses, two temple halls, and a new main bridge and gate at its northwest corner, the Ōtemon-*bashi*. Ienobu improved on his successor's work and, shortly after his inauguration, celebrated the completion of the island—it was surrounded by moats and walls—by landing a festively decorated boat at its new bayside mooring.

Inheriting the Hama-*goten* from the *bakufu*, the Meiji government decided to use it as a venue for state visits. They renamed it the Hama-*rikyū*, or 'Beach Imperial Villa,' and to accommodate the foreign guests built a new, Western-style, brick-and-

mortar villa called the Enryō-kan, on its premises. Over the next two decades, a string of foreign dig-

nitaries (including American president Ulysses Grant) retreated to the park-like sanctuary after a busy day of official engagements in Tokyo and elsewhere.

Today, the island is just that: a green sanctuary amid Tokyo's high-octane business district. Now called the Hama-rikyū Gardens, it was designated

a Special National Historic Site in 1952. And though the **Enryō**-*kan* is no more, a small shrine, the Inabu-

jinja, and four of its tea houses—the Nakajima no Ochaya (1983), the Matsu no Ochaya (2010), the **Tsubame no Ochaya** (2015), and the Taka no

Ochaya (2018)—have since been rebuilt. The *shōgun*'s mooring place is still in place, as are the massive foundations of the Ōte-*mon* gate.

Tsukiji Hongan-ji

Just left of the Hama-*goten* on Beato's panorama, one can clearly see the **massive roof of the Tsukiji Hongan-***ji*. It was a branch temple of the Nishi (West) and Higashi (East) Hongan temple complexes just north of Kyoto's central station. They were and are home to the famed Jōdō Shinshū or True Pure Land sect of Buddhism The great warlord Oda Nobunaga would have taken exception to the term 'famed,' for he spent the better part of a decade fighting their fanatic *sōhei*, or 'warrior monks,' at their Ishiyama Hongan-*ji* temple complex near Osaka.

The Tsukiji Hongan-*ji* was built in 1617, long after Japan's Buddhist sects had abandoned their opposition to centralized rule and the warrior monks had returned to their religious duties. Its original location was farther north, at Higashi-Nihonbashi, on the west bank of the Sumida River. That temple was destroyed in the Great Fire of Meireki, in 1657, when much of Edo's eastern part was laid in ashes and a quarter of its citizens lost their lives. It may have been because the fire started at one of Edo's temples that the *bakufu* forced the temple, along with many other religious buildings to relocate (legend has it that the fire was started by a priest of the Honmyō Temple when he set fire to a kimono of a young girl who had fallen in love with one of its monks). The Tsukiji Hongan-*ji* was rebuilt in 1679, but this time on a plot of reclaimed land near Tsukudashima (today's Tsukuda in Tokyo's Chūō Ward).

The temple remained untouched by the other 1700-odd fires that visited the capital during the Edo period. It stood right up until the Great Kantō Earthquake of 1923. Its massive structure survived the 7.9 magnitude shock, but was nevertheless reduced to cinders when city fires broke out in the wake of the earthquake.

Plans were soon underway to rebuild the temple. But not in wood. The sect's high priest, Count Ōtani Kōzui, had something quite different in mind. Kōzui was a fervent explorer and had financed as well as taken part in several archeological expeditions to China and India to do research into historic Buddhist sites. He had come away with a deep appreciation of India's architecture and wanted to implement it in the reconstruction of his sect's destroyed branch temple in Tokyo. And so he engaged his friend the professor of architecture at Tokyo's Imperial University, Itō Chūta, whom he had met on his first expedition, to design a new

building inspired by India's three major religions using modern steel-reinforced concrete. The result was a celebration of India's architectural traditions,

combining Buddhist, Hindu, and Islam influences in an imposing palatial blend in tune with Japan's then-imperial aspirations.

TOKYO – Tsukiji Hongan-ji

Edo-jō

An even more exciting view from Atago-*yama*'s crest is presented in a newly discovered photograph from the early 1870s. It was taken by the Austrian photographer Michael Moser. Moser had come to Japan in 1869 and had been allowed to settle in Tokyo when he was hired by the Meiji government as a photographer and interpreter. Moser's image is doubly exciting as it is a so-called stereoscopic photograph, in which two images, taken at slightly different angles, create the illusion of three-dimensional depth when viewed through a stereoscope. It was taken from Atago-*yama*'s northern crest toward Hibiya and, in the far distance, the elevated grounds of Edo Castle.

In the foreground, one looks down on the roofs of one of the compounds of Mōri Motozumi, the last *daimyō* of the Kiyosue domain in Chōshū Province (Yamaguchi Prefecture). It sat right next to the Shinpuku-*ji*, a small temple at the northeast foot of the hill. Toward the left of the image(s), one can see the long white buildings of the Kōgaku-*ryō*, the forerunner of the Imperial College of

Engineering. They sat on a stretch of reclaimed wetlands that bordered the castle on the south. Its main point of access was the Tora-*no-mon*. The semi-island was also the home to the Imperial Army's Hibiya training grounds. Established in 1871,

they were the place where the Japanese emperor would inspect the troops. It was only a short trot on horseback for the monarch, who only four years earlier had moved into a newly built Imperial Palace

(Kōkyo) within the castle's former western bailey (Nishi-*no-maru*). In the far distance (right of center in the left-hand image and on the right in the right-hand image) one can just make out the white running turret (*watari-yagura*) that graced the high castle wall between the western bailey's Shoin Gate and its two-story Fushimi Turret. Both guarded the Nijū Bridge. *Nijū* means 'two-layers,' referring to the bridge's unique double-decked structure.

Edo Castle at this juncture, was already rapidly changing, and not only because its grounds were being repurposed by the military. Many structures that had survived the countless city fires of the Edo period were lost during the early Meiji period in yet more fires. Among them were the second bailey's multi-storied Hasuike- and Hasuike-Tatsumi-*yagura*. Another huge blow to the castle's surviving structures came in 1873, when the vast *goten* within the grounds of the Nishi-no-maru burned down.

Exactly a decade earlier, the *goten* within the inner citadel had also been destroyed by fire. Neither were rebuilt. The wooden Nijū-*bashi*, too, was lost. It was replaced by a cast-iron bridge designed by the German civil engineer Georg Heinrich Wilhelm

Left: Edo Castle's Shoin-mon and Nijū-*bashi*, with in the background a Fushimi-*yagura* in scaffolding

Below: Today's Fushimi-*yagura*, with in the foreground the Seimon Ishi-*bashi* and, just visible behind it, the Seimon Tetsu-*bashi*

Heise in 1888. The **present cast-iron bridge**, formally called the Deimon Nijū-bashi, took the place of the Seimon Tetsu-*bashi* in 1964 when the old imperial palace was replaced by a new one.

The many late-*Bakufu* and early-Meiji photographs reveal a castle as it had existed for more than two centuries. They are now a major source of information for historians and architects alike. Indeed, it was the photographs of the early Meiji period (taken at a time when the castle layout was no longer militarily classified) that provided the data on which many of the castle's present structures—among them the Fushimi-, Fujimi-, and Tatsumi-*yagura*—have been rebuit.

Nevertheless, Edo Castle has undergone profound changes since those early foreign and Japanese photographers set up their tripods in and around its grounds, as has its city, as has Japan. As such, the castle has become a symbol of both the losses that Japanese cultural heritage has suf-

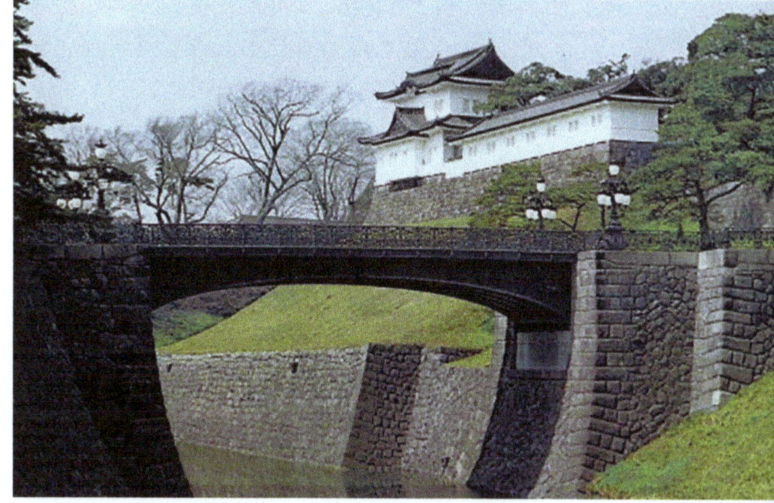

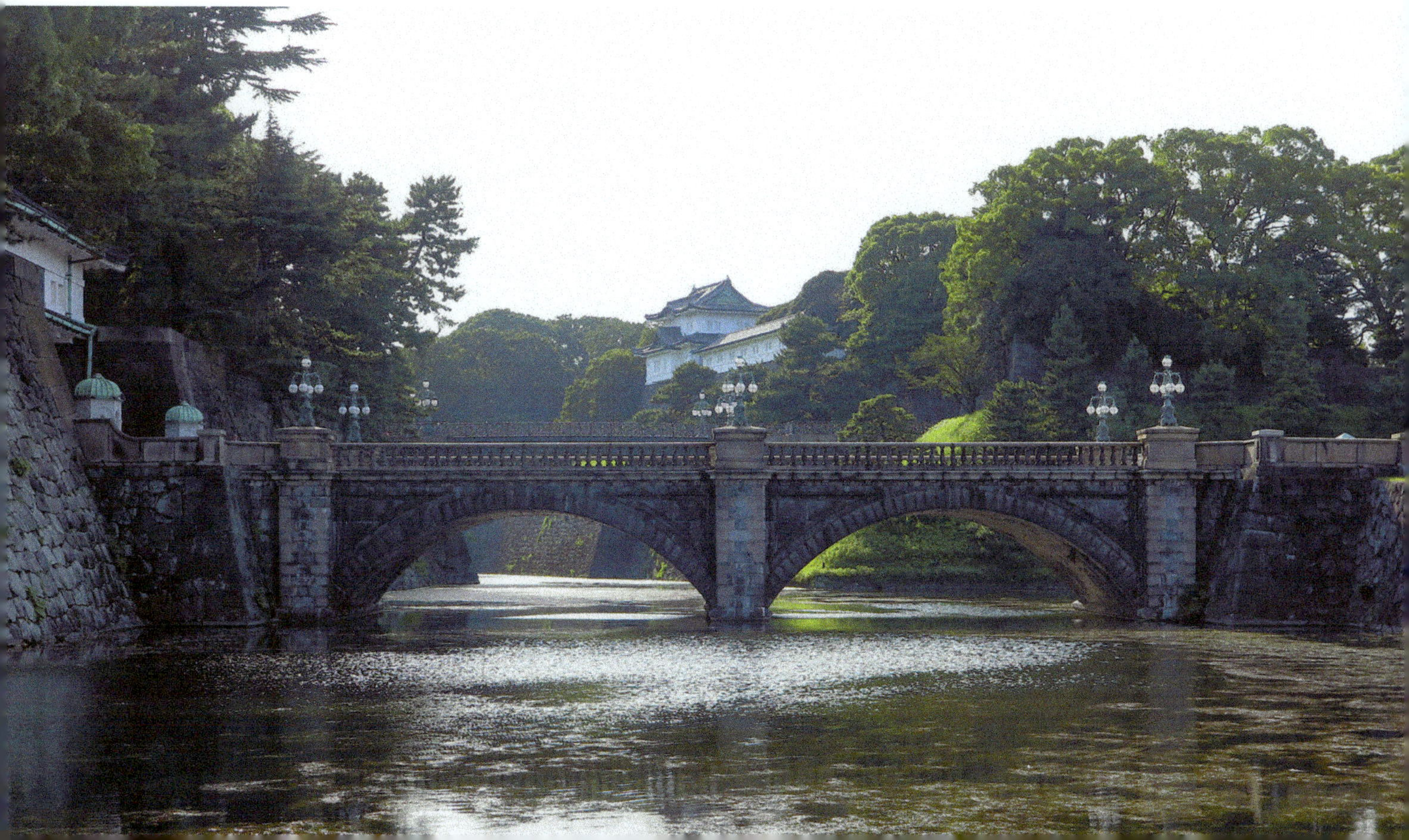

fered since the end of the Edo period, but also the efforts to restore and preserve the great number of structures and sites that have been saved.

Michael Moser (1853–1912) was born into a family from Altaussee, Austria. When, in 1867, the Vienna photographer Wilhelm Burger approached his father (who supplemented his meager income as a salt miner by doing woodwork) to make him a tripod, he was impressed with the boy's diligence and agreed to take him on as an apprentice. Moser learned fast and when, the next year, Burger was selected as the official photographer with the Imperial Austrian Mission to East Asia and South America, he brought the young Moser along as his assistant.

The mission arrived in Yokohama on 2 October 1869. When, having successfully negotiated treaties with Japan, it sailed again on 14 November, the young Moser decided to stay behind. With no money and no knowledge of the Japanese language, he spent an uncertain few months as a waiter in a local *izakaya*. Moser's prospects brightened when the local Scottish publisher John Reddie Black hired him as a photographer for his publications.

During the next few years, Moser traveled Japan making photographs for Black's magazine *The Far East*. At the same time, he learned the Japanese language, as well as English and Italian, which in turn landed him a position as an interpreter for the Japanese delegation to the World Exhibition in Vienna in 1873.

Returning to Japan overland via Nepal (he hated sailing), Moser was hired by the Meiji government as a photographer, in which capacity he was introduced to the Meiji emperor and his consort. His linguistic and photographic talents also earned him a place in the Japanese delegation to the 1876 Centennial Exhibition in Philadelphia. During his stay in America Moser contracted typhoid fever and, on his eventual recovery, decided to return home, where he married fellow photographer Franziska Fruhwirth.

The couple settled down in Bad Aussee, where they ran a photographic studio until his death at the age of fifty-nine.

INDEX

TOYO PRess publishes books that contribute to a deeper understanding of Asian cultures. Book and cover design: Chōkei Studios. Editorial supervision: Letitia van der Merwe. Printing and binding: IngramSpark. The typeface is Avenir.